www.peakyclimbers.com

PEAKY
CLIMBERS

How eight amateur cyclists became kings of the mountains

Paul McIntosh with Anna Hughes

BROWN
DOG
BOOKS

First published 2018

Published under licence by Brown Dog Books and The Self-Publishing Partnership, 7 Green Park Station, Bath BA1 1JB

www.selfpublishingpartnership.co.uk

ISBN printed book: 978-1-78545-333-5
ISBN e-book: 978-1-78545-334-2

Cover design by Kevin Rylands
Internal design by Andrew Easton
Daily route profile maps by Simon Warren

Printed and bound by CPI Group (UK) Ltd, Croydon, CR0 4YY

Dedicated to the memory of
Maisie Norton and Valerie McIntosh

Profits from the sale of this book will be donated to the
Caring Cancer Trust and the British Lung Foundation.
Thank you for supporting these causes that are very
close to our hearts.

Maisie Norton 1998 - 2015

Valerie McIntosh 1939 - 2007

Caring Cancer Trust:
Reg Charity No: 1052205

British Lung Foundation:
Registered charity in England and
Wales (326730), Scotland (038415)
and the Isle of Man (1177)

Contents

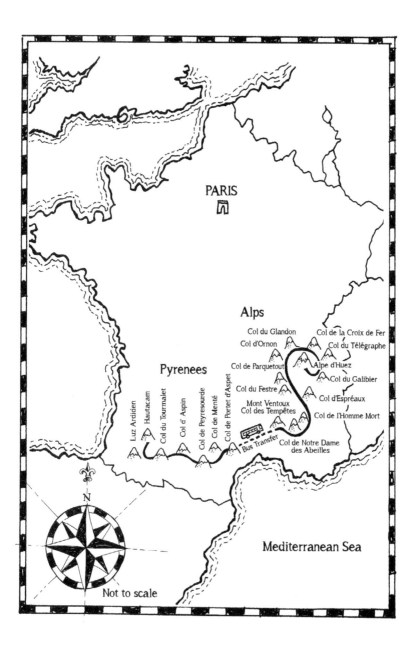

PARIS

Alps

Col du Glandon   Col de la Croix de Fer
Col d'Ornon   Col du Télégraphe
Col de Parquetout   Alpe d'Huez
Pyrenees   Col du Galibier
Col du Festre   Col d'Espréaux
Mont Ventoux   Col de l'Homme Mort
Col des Tempêtes

Luz Ardiden
Hautacam
Col du Tourmalet
Col d' Aspin
Col de Peyresourde
Col de Menté
Col de Portet d'Aspet

Bus Transfer   Col de Notre Dame
des Abeilles

N

Mediterranean Sea

Not to scale

9

Prologue

Col = a mountain pass

It is not the mountain we conquer, but ourselves
Edmund Hillary

The road rises snake-like ahead, tarmac shimmering and sun-heated in the distance. A series of zig-zags leads steadily upwards, shaking off the clutches of the sheep-scattered valley. Patches of pines stand in isolation as the road emerges above the tree line, vegetation growing sparse between the exposed rocks. Breaths come in deep, steady gasps, filling the head, while hearts thud in ears. Thighs burn and feet spin, hands grip bars, dragging the body upwards. As the incline steepens the chain clunks heavily into the lowest gear; the only tactic that remains is to stand in the pedals, the full force of the body striving upwards, running on the bike, the frame swaying in a broken rhythm beneath.

The view opens up as the rider ventures ever higher, peaks on all sides, a sprinkling of snow on the tallest, a scene of breathtaking grandeur. It is humbling to creep through such landscapes, and all thoughts of proving strength and satisfying the ego are lost: it is in climbing mountains that we discover how insignificant we really are.

There are two choices: to maintain the upward trajectory or turn around and retreat. In edging beyond the comfort zone we stretch ourselves, learn our true limits, expand our physical, mental and emotional capabilities. It is more than simply reaching the peak: climbing mirrors how we tackle the challenges of our daily lives, chipping away at those seemingly insurmountable problems, persevering, breaking the task into manageable chunks, dealing with the immediate as it approaches. In return we gain satisfaction, freedom and an overwhelming sense of achievement.

The magnificence of the mountains has called people from age to age, from explorer to tourist, adventurer to sportsman. There is so much that is unique about such landscapes, a place where the view evolves with each mile, where upward effort is followed by freewheeling reward, where the lack of human habitation means slopes teem with wildlife. Full of beauty, and of indescribable scale, this presents the ultimate challenge: those who climb mountains can do anything.

Day One

Luz-Saint-Sauveur – Luz-Saint-Sauveur

Distance 94km Elevation gain 3553m

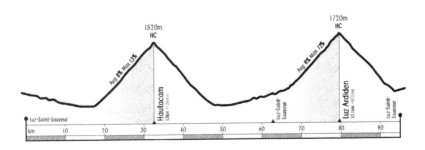

The Tour de France has always been an item in the sporting calendar that grabs my attention. All sports do, really: football to re-live my 'glory' days of managing a local amateur team; cricket because my dad was always dragging us to his matches when we were young; rugby because of the bullish but gentlemanly teamwork on display. But cycling is different. There is something entrancing about a group of athletes racing through the stunning landscape of France, an element of danger, tactics and skill, but above all a huge show of strength. It is incredibly impressive, multi-day racing, to hit the road at speed and to sustain it for days on end. And the mountain climbs – those are something else. Watching riders ascend grabs me more than any of the rest of it. You can see the pain etched on their faces, you can see the exhaustion rolling through their bodies yet still they climb, determined not to let the slope beat them. Something in me wanted a piece of it.

A sports enthusiast, I played football well into my forties, tried my hand at running, then turned to golf when middle-age spread hit. I never saw myself as a cyclist. But in my mid-forties, I took part in the London 100 sportive; raising money by riding a bike seemed to be the done thing. It was bloody tough but I actually enjoyed it. So I joined the local social cycling club and caught the bug. Fast forward four years and, with seven others who have become dear friends as we've made our preparations, we're about to take on the most difficult challenge any of us has ever faced: to cycle 20 peaks of the Tour de France in seven days.

So, picture the professional peloton. Matching jerseys, off the scale expensive bikes, in their team the climber, the sprinter, the general dogsbody or *domestique*. All at the absolute peak of fitness, primed for the task ahead, accompanied by an entourage of support vehicles, nutritionists, coaches, mechanics, spare wheels, spare bikes, and a carefully calculated daily allowance of calories. It might be supposed, then, that the mountains are the domain only of riders whose Lycra doesn't sag around a midriff, whose training regime wasn't made up in the pub, and who have spent months in high altitudes acclimatising and preparing. Enter the Peaky Climbers.

Introducing the team we have:

Mark 'Cricky' Crick, a big-hearted bear of a guy, the kind whose smile never leaves his rough-shaven face – especially if it's on camera. Never short on confidence, he's a nifty climber and generally strong cyclist, and is the joker of the bunch, though the joke is often on him.

Allen Stacey, a pocket rocket and a true gentleman who will always put the needs of the team before his own. Allen has been assigned the role of Head Mechanic and Health and Safety officer.

John 'JB' Boaler, a Tigger-like character with massive energy and boundless enthusiasm. He maintains that the mid-ride pint makes him a better cyclist.

Simon Haly, a pub landlord who brims with enthusiasm and humour. At several stone heavier than Chris Froome he's not a natural climber but is a hurricane on the descents.

Ben Heavers, at 34 years old the youngest of the team, even less built for climbing than Simon but with more willpower to reach the peak than any of us.

Neil 'Nobby' Barson, our poster boy. He's the top climber among us, and would be in the polka dot jersey if it weren't for the late addition of…

Graham Cherrill, the most capable cyclist of us all. Any opportunity for a long bike ride or a challenge, he's there, especially if there's a glass of red to be enjoyed at the end. We've appointed Graham as our domestique, essentially riding to help the rest of us out – there's no point in making it any easier on him than it needs to be.

And finally, me, Paul 'Macca' McIntosh, the one who hoodwinked all the guys into this in the first place. Team skipper but by no means the best cyclist, I can just about keep up with the fellas, though I do like a climb.

At least we have the matching jerseys.

It is often said that getting to the start line is the most difficult part of any challenge. Since the idea first came into my head, it has been two years of dreaming, 18 months of planning and a solid year of training, tears, tensions, pains, strains, neglected wives and re-prioritised lives. But here we are, in southern France, about to embark upon our pilgrimage. Part of my thought process is of disbelief. At so many points I had feared we wouldn't make it, had worried that the task I had set us all was too much. But overwhelmingly it is of gratification: despite all the doubters, despite the fact that not one of our team has ever done anything of this magnitude before, we are here. All the preparation has been done: now we just have to go out there and ride. Though not a particularly emotional guy, there is a definite lump in my throat as we line up for the photograph. I couldn't be more proud.

Mark seems to have forgotten his kit: he is dressed in a short-sleeved jersey, fingerless gloves and the smallest cycling shorts the world has ever seen.

'What's with the speedos, Cricky?'

'Best thing for this weather, mate.'

The sky hangs heavy with clouds, the road dotted with puddles from the overnight rainfall.

'Skin's waterproof, I suppose.'

We tease Mark for a while over his kit selection until I bring them all to attention with, 'OK Peaky Climbers, it's time.'

One by one bicycles are mounted, and with feet clipped, we roll into the valley. Thirty seconds later the rain starts.

This is not what we had imagined when we signed up to a South of France challenge, but at this stage, nothing can dampen our spirits. Our wheels glide over the glistening tarmac as we ride into the downpour, with a sense of 'bring it on'. Peaks rise in all directions, a corrugated skyline of mountains, some completely covered with mist, some with slopes visible through the clouds. The land surrounding the river is a rich green, a mass of vegetation which creeps upwards onto lower slopes swathed in conifers and beech. Ahead, way in the distance, are the mountains that will be climbed over the course of the next few days.

It's 17 kilometres to the foot of the first climb: Hautacam, meaning *High Land*. We charge down the road like a raucous group of lads at a party, jeering, laughing, joking with each other, affectionate insults flowing as fast as our wheels. All the while the rain hammers, soaking us through, with a smattering of wind added for extra spice. Arms and thighs take the hit as mudguard-free tyres spin down the road, the verge surging with water, eyes blinking against the spray. The rain lends a grey tinge to the countryside as we follow the river, ticking off the kilometres until the road will rise up to the first mountain climb. It's stoic riding, ignoring the downpour, though not even banter can stave off the cold.

'I think there's something wrong with my bike,' says Graham. 'It's wobbling.'

'That's you shivering.'

'I'm freezing already and we haven't even started climbing!' says Nobby. 'How are we going to last seven days of this?'

'Forget the Hautacam; we have to get up Tourmalet tomorrow!'

'One climb at a time, fellas,' I say, adapting a line from my football managing days. 'Take it one climb at a time.'

'Come on,' says Mark, pushing forward. 'Let's get cracking on this first col.'

We surge along the road, buzzing with excitement and a fair amount of trepidation. None of us can quite comprehend that the challenge is finally here: we are really doing it, riding these peaks, bringing to life our own little *Tour de France*, our own King of the Mountains.

The Hautacam rises to 1520m, a giant of the Midi-Pyrénées. It's an occasional player in the Tour de France, and is labelled as *HC – hors-catégorie* – beyond categorisation, in other words bloody difficult. It is the kind of mountain that cracked five-time Tour winner Miguel Induráin, and was the scene of one of Lance Armstrong's more memorable moments: in the 2000 Tour, as he launched his steady decimation of the field, eliminating the 10 minute lead of his competitor, his team manager reportedly told him to slow down so as not to arouse suspicion.

After soaking us thoroughly for more than an hour, the rain finally stops; jackets are removed as we reach the turning for the climb, which will wriggle its way through open pasture towards the summit ski resort. The road is quiet after the bustle of the valley, and villages come and go, a collection of balconied, white-walled buildings with dark slate roofs and shutters thrown open, hemmed in by stone walls.

This is a much-practised routine: we split into pairs and head on up the slope. Leading the pack are Mark and Nobby; having gone on many cycling adventures together, these two have naturally fallen into a riding partnership. They've known each other for years, and their wives, both called Jane, are similarly close – more so, in fact, as they don't bicker half as much as their husbands. Mark's the loud half of the relationship, though Nobby does like a good laugh. With natural athleticism that makes the rest of us a tiny bit envious, they make short work of the incline, soon disappearing out of sight.

Allen and Ben are next, following at a good lick. These two have been soul-mates since day one of training, since Ben had a blowout and Head Mechanic Allen came to the rescue. Their sense of humour matches, Ben's just a big kid in need of some affection, and Allen is one of the most generous-hearted men you'll ever meet. They make good roommates too: Ben snores like a train and Allen sleeps like he's in a coma.

JB and I follow. It just so happens that we've fallen into a climbing partnership, which was a surprise to both of us; in the early days of training, JB would typically be leading the pack with Mark while I sat at the rear (riding fast on the flat is not my strong point, and I could see the rest of the team from that position – that was my excuse, anyway). But we match each other well in the climbing stakes. We've been good buddies for a while, having met on a mutual friend's skiing trip and kept in touch. 'Statto' is the team's pet name for JB. A lover of statistics, he has collected every little fact we might need to make our trip a success, including topography maps of each ascent, so he's our go-to guy for information.

Simon has settled into the climb behind us, with Graham there to keep him company. Simon is what some might call a 'proper' cyclist, riding with Devon CTC back in the day, but managing a busy pub does not allow much time for exercise and he's now carrying enough weight to make those climbs tricky. His willpower and determination, however, have become legendary. Even though he's often the last to summit, watching him crest the ridge having worked so hard to get there, and still with a massive smile on his face, is fast becoming a favourite Peaky moment. Simon talks a great game and makes everyone feel positive; the opposite of Graham, in fact, whom we often tease for never smiling. That's not to say he's not a good guy; the most recent addition to the Peaky Climbers, and perfectly capable of zooming up these climbs, he's become invaluable in supporting those who need it.

The slope kicks in. Down a gear – *clunk* – down one more – *clunk* – and with the next clunk the chain shifts onto the smallest chainring and our bicycles can provide no further help. Now it's a case of finding a rhythm and settling into the climb for the next hour and a half. Signposts by the side of the road tick off the kilometres and show the gradient, which varies dramatically. After a section of respite the roller coaster ramps into double figures and we're faced with a gradient that tops one in ten for a good stint. Steadily, inch by inch, we grind our way to the top. Behind us, the settlements retreat into the folds of the hillside, the river valley appearing far below, hazy in the lingering damp. Jackets are replaced as the rain resumes, the teasing skies soaking nearly-dry jerseys through once more. The slope eases off for the final two kilometres and with an easier gradient and the surging adrenaline that comes with having almost reached our first peak, we race towards the vast car park and deserted ski station, where we regroup so we can cross the summit line together.

'Is this it?'

Ben rolls to a stop in front of the Hautacam sign, disappointment on his face. I don't know what we were expecting – fireworks and fanfares, maybe? The inaugural col was built up to be something major, something momentous, so to find a deserted car park and a view half hidden by rain clouds is a bit of an anticlimax. But soon the euphoria of completing Col Number One kicks in and relief and happiness sweep over the entire team. There are hugs, high fives and lots of back slapping, and with smiles on our faces we take our first summit team photo.

With jackets zipped, the descent begins: the sweat of the climb will quickly cool. It's a return along the roads by which the ascent was made, and though we know what is coming it feels entirely different, the hard-won kilometres flitting by in a blur. Those hairpins that we cursed our way around are treacherous in the rain. Allen and I are cautious on the brakes, not wishing the challenge to be over too soon, and Nobby, who hates a descent, carefully follows. But the risk takers of the pack, Ben and Simon, are long gone. Those two are definitely more built for the downhill, and race each other to the bottom.

'Bloody sheep!'

There had been some sheep watching the ascent with interest, standing motionless on the bend, and as the pack leaders pass at speed, the sheep decide now is the perfect time to cross.

Back in the river valley, it's a hyper-charged 18 kilometres to Luz-Saint-Sauveur, the buzz of the first summit lingering. Lunch, kit check, refill bottles. It's only day one and already the machine is looking well-oiled. The first climb is over, the initial test passed. Now is the time to relax and enjoy it. Only 19 peaks to go.

It was almost two years ago that the idea for this challenge began to take shape. A thought niggled at the back of my mind that I was approaching my 50s, and I needed to do something momentous. A mid-life crisis would usually involve a Porsche or a new fitness regime, and with the missus forbidding the car (something about looking ridiculous in a Porsche, never mind looking ridiculous on a bike) exercise was the only option.

But just a gym membership wouldn't suffice – I needed to do something monumental, something huge, something that would significantly impact my life and change it for the better.

More of an incentive was the 10th anniversary of my mother's death. She had suffered from idiopathic pulmonary fibrosis (IPF), a degenerative lung disease that, ten years on, still has no cure. If I could raise a substantial amount of money for the British Lung Foundation and increase awareness of the disease by taking on a challenge, that would be a considerable help and a meaningful token of remembrance.

Other cycle challenges such as Land's End to John o' Groats (LEJOG) were considered, but none had the weight or drama that I desired. Looming in the back of my mind were the Pyrenees, the mountains that I had always admired while watching the Tour de France on TV, and in which I had spent many happy hours – my wife Nicola and I had spent a substantial amount of time there working on property renovation projects. Each time we travelled to the south of France and drove the cols I would picture myself cycling each one. Slowly an idea formed: to ride the biggest peaks of the Tour in the Alps and the Pyrenees. It ticked all the boxes: a physical challenge; a kick-start to fitness; a beautiful part of the world of which I was very fond; and a difficult enough project that I hoped would attract a substantial amount of sponsorship. The speed with which Mum's disease took her from us had brought everything into sharp focus. No one knows what's around the corner, so we must take these opportunities while we can, and seize the day. There was no better time than now.

A quick internet search revealed the companies that might support such a venture. This would be crucial for its success: to have the logistics worked out by people who knew what they were doing, so I could focus my efforts on fundraising and training. One company, Le Domestique Cycle Tours, ran a week-long challenge – the *King of the Mountains* – which would take on the highest peaks that were on my list, with the small matter of linking them all together with hundreds of kilometres of cycling and several other 'minor' cols (each of those still being higher than anything in the UK). The tour operator would provide support vans and would be in charge of route, accommodation and transfers. It was exactly what I had been looking for. I saw it as akin to starting a business. I had an idea, drew up a plan, worked out how much it would cost, sourced the funding, and began to put together a team.

The attack on the lower slopes of our second climb, Luz Ardiden, coincides with the heavens opening once more. It had been warm, a brief break in the clouds allowing some respite, but with the sky now greying over, the temperature plummets. Beneath a canopy of leaves we climb. It's steady but tough, the endless switchbacks climbing ever skywards at an incline of 10%, easy enough at first glance but after several kilometres, legs and lungs are burning.

'Alright, Skip?' says Mark, swinging past as he leads out the climb.

Despite the water dripping into my eyes I turn to him with a huge grin.

'Top notch, Cricky. Never better.'

And I mean it: no matter how cold and soaked we are, I wouldn't change this for the world.

The road is scrawled with the ubiquitous graffiti from the Tour de France, chalked encouragement from fans which remains tattooed on the road long after the race is over. It's hard to imagine now, as we crawl up the mountain, the crowds spilling into the road, cheering and screaming, gesturing in riders' faces and parting only at the last second. It's one of the curiosities of the Tour that fans are permitted to get up close and personal with riders with no barriers to hold them back. In a rare breach of the spectator/rider agreement, the great Belgian Eddy Merckx was punched in the stomach, and it was on these very slopes that Armstrong was brought to the ground by a stray handbag strap. Though his rivals in the peloton neutralised their attack, Armstrong saw red, his blood boiling with rage and, as we now know, the performance-enhancing drug EPO. He chased down the pack and picked them off one by one to win the climb and his fifth Tour. The roads are quiet now, in the graffiti the ghosts lingering in the air, the occasional passing vehicle the only thing to break the rhythm of the climb.

Mark Crick was one of the first team members to come on board. The chairman of local cycling club Grench – named after Grove and Denchworth, two villages in the mid-Oxfordshire countryside – he's the type who is always looking for the next challenge, the tougher the better. I'd known him for a while as he'd played the odd football match for me back when I managed Milton United Veterans, where, in that cruel yet affectionate way that blokes do, we gave him the nickname 'Polo' for the times we passed him the ball and it went right through him. He's a big guy, but so is Miguel Induráin and look what he achieved: five Tour wins and two in the Giro d'Italia. It was doing the Three Peaks challenge with a group from work a decade previously that sparked Mark's enthusiasm for endurance events and the great outdoors. Two London marathons followed, then the LEJOG bike ride and the Ireland End to End with Nobby. Mark is now a confirmed cycling nut. He would ride every day if he could.

It was an innocuous Sunday afternoon when we bumped into each other at a charity football match at Wantage Town.

'Cricky!'

'Hiya mate.'

'Listen, I'm planning a cycling challenge for next summer, to ride 20 peaks from the Tour de France in seven days. I need a team to ride with – are you up for it?'

Barely waiting for the detail, he agreed. 'Sounds crackers, mate. Count me in. Nobby will probably do it, too.'

Being Mark's partner in crime, Nobby took similarly little persuading. A regular cyclist and of slight build, he was a dead cert for a climbing challenge. The team was beginning to shape up.

The tree cover recedes to reveal a stunning panorama of peaks. A wall of mountains punches into the horizon on each side, the Pyrenean giants guarding the Spanish border in the distance. Yet another deserted ski station looms ahead, the chairs dangling uselessly above summer slopes bare of snow, announcing the Luz Ardiden summit. Mark and Nobby are already settled there, energy bars in hand; any chance to get some food down must be taken.

Ben arrives and leans back on his bike, taking in the view and breathing great lungfuls of crisp Pyrenean air. 'Bloody hell. This is more like it. Just take a look at that.' It feels as though we can see the whole world.

'Good climb, everyone?' I ask.

'Great.' Simon is grinning from ear to ear.

'Someone give JB a gag! He wouldn't stop singing all the way up,' says Graham.

'It's for motivation, mate! You love it.'

The usually taciturn Graham makes a wisecrack in return and we all roar with laughter – he doesn't generally join in with the banter, but the mountain air has obviously done something to him and he's now fully inducted into the Peaky ways. There's something about a group of men on bikes that brings out the childish. We're merciless towards each other, no weakness left unacknowledged, no slack cut for anyone. It's a delicate balance of outright mickey-taking and genuine affection that has only increased as we've got to know each other. Each member of the team gets their fair share of grief, which is an integral part of the challenge – with the freedom of the road comes a loosening of the tongue, and the camaraderie that taking on the mountains instils is reflected in the way we communicate. It's tactical, too. By shifting the focus from the climbs the pain is reduced, and the odd guffaw gives some respite as we try to suck in more air.

It's a spectacular view back down the climb, an endless snake of switchbacks ribboning up the slopes. It seems almost impossible that we just climbed it. But once again, we must descend, a reversal of the way we came up.

'Not too fast now, boys,' says JB.

'Yes, Dad,' replies Ben before disappearing over the precipice.

Allen tuts at this blatant lack of caution. He wasn't named Health and Safety officer for nothing.

Back down to earth, the first day is complete. We herd into the hotel, soaked through and freezing, peeling off wet layers to be washed and dried by the hotel staff, feeling like boys on a school trip. It's part holiday, part adventure, and we're pumped with adrenaline as we coax fingers back to life in the shower; with the effort, the emotions, the excitement and the nerves comes the euphoria of completing day one, and the trepidation for what is yet to come. Our bikes have been stored in the hotel's night club ('They must have heard we cut a mean rug on the dance floor,' says JB). There follows that first feast of the challenge, when the word 'hungry' just won't do. Conversation and beers flow easily and we put away an unreal amount of food. None of us will have trouble sleeping tonight.

Day Two

Luz-Saint-Sauveur – Bagnères-de-Luchon

Distance 107km Elevation gain 3984m

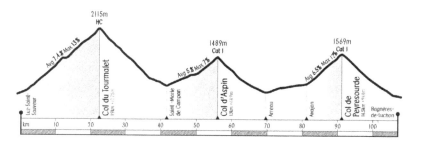

'You alright, Mark?'

Mark and Nobby are partway up the Col du Tourmalet, the first climb of the day. The road curves around the mountainside with a sheer drop to the right. Mark does not look happy. His usual grin is gone and his eyes are fixed on the tarmac in too-keen concentration. He is riding on the wrong side of the road, as far away from the edge as he can.

'Vertigo,' he replies through gritted teeth.

'Good one, mate!' Nobby laughs. No one would agree to climb 20 mountains if they suffered from vertigo. But on this narrow road, with an almost non-existent verge that falls sharply towards the valley floor and no barrier to hold them in, there's no hiding. Mark's breaths are snatched and shallow, and in his frown is the definite look of fear.

'Oh. You're serious. Shit.'

None of us knew Mark suffered this badly. Having never done anything like this, he probably didn't know it himself. But it's becoming a significant problem: if this continues, he will never make it up the mountain.

'OK, talk to me. Tell me about your boys. What are they up to?'

Breath. 'Ruben might be out for a run. He's started,' breath, 'running half marathons since I signed up for this.' Breath. 'Harrison is probably out with Jane. He's off to university soon,' breath, 'so she said she'd take him shopping. He's actually moving out in a few days. It's bad timing with me out here and Jane flying out at the end of the week, because we won't be there to help him.' Breath. 'I feel terrible about that. We're missing such a major moment in his life.'

'I know what you mean. Life goes on even though we're doing this. Bet they're both proud of you though.'

A smile. 'Yep. They're really chuffed. They think I'm totally mad. Right now I agree with them.'

For the next few kilometres they talk, Nobby asking questions, telling terrible jokes, anything to distract Mark from the drop. They inch their way up the mountain.

It's freezing. Yesterday's rain continued long into the morning and we were completely saturated by the time the climb even began, the snaking road surging with water, our limbs heavy beneath soaking wet Lycra. Mark, though, has remained in those shorts. It's beginning to look as though that's the only kit he brought, which comes as no surprise – he's a complete chancer, always underprepared – although when we checked the weather forecast before coming out here, at no point did it suggest it would be this cold and wet. Nobby only brought a winter jacket as an afterthought. Throughout all the training, in the tedium of those long winter rides through the cold and dark, we would look forward to the good summer weather of the south of France. No one had anticipated these conditions.

JB and I have fallen into our usual partnership. Today, his songs are of a theme: 'Why does it always rain on me?', 'Raindrops keep falling on my head', and anything by *Wet Wet Wet*.

Our support team from Le Domestique has been doing a terrific job. Pete, driving one of the vans, has spent the first few climbs driving ahead, monitoring how we're doing and giving us everything we need. Jack is in the other van. Ostensibly his job is to check our lunch stops and accommodation, but given the weather we have a suspicion he might have just headed straight to the next pub. At the village of Barèges we come to a stop next to the van, where Nobby and Mark are waiting for everyone to regroup. A couple of locals approach.

'Are you seriously aiming for the top?' they ask. 'There is no way you'll make it – have you seen the snow?'

'What snow?'

They point towards the summit, which is just visible through the clouds. It is covered entirely in white.

'Er, guys,' Mark says as the rest of the team pulls up. 'It's looking a bit dodgy up there.'

'I know, a German couple just pulled over to warn us about the conditions,' Ben says, breathlessly coming to a halt.

Simon squints towards the clouds. 'Do you think we can make it?'

Allen quietly watches the discussion. It's clear from his face that he has doubts.

'Well, it's fine here,' says Ben. 'I reckon we keep going and see how far we get.'

'Either way, I'm ruddy freezing, so can we make a decision and get going, please?' Nobby is visibly shivering. Like Mark, he's only wearing cycling shorts.

'Regretting the speedos are we now, boys?'

We press on.

Through the air floats the sound of a farmer whistling and calling his dogs, and distant bells growing steadily louder. Upwards we ride then, rounding a corner, we slam on the brakes. Blocking the road is a maelstrom of sheep jostling each other down the hill. There must be a hundred at least. There is nowhere to go – it's impossible even to pull over, and we dismount and stand stock still with our bikes, helplessly trapped like islands in the middle of a surging tide of fleece. It's a huge, jangling cacophony, each animal wearing a clanging bell around its neck. They barge into each other, eyeing us with wild, wary eyes. It's unnerving, and we grow colder as we stand there, with no choice but to wait. Finally they are gone and as the circus recedes we resume our ride. While cyclists climb mountains, farmers continue to farm.

This climb holds particular meaning for me. It was on a family camping holiday in the region many moons ago that Nicola and I attempted to drive to the summit with Jai and Ethan, our two young sons. A dramatic change in the weather partway up reduced the visibility to barely past the bonnet of our Volvo estate. Not being an especially manoeuvrable motor, it was a lengthy 23 point turn before we could retreat to ground level. The next day we tried again, but this time were thwarted by a herd of goats being brought down the hill, necessitating another 47 point turn. We finally managed it on the third time of asking. It seems that reaching the summit of this mountain is destined to always be challenged by weather and livestock.

More significantly, it was on this very mountain that I received the phone call the day before Mum died. It had been a quick trip to sign some paperwork for one of the renovation projects we were working on, but the day I landed I received the news that she might not last much longer. After a sleepless night and an early morning flight it was a furious drive down the M4 at many miles per hour over the speed limit to make it to the Hospice. I was 40 minutes away when my brother called with the awful news that she had passed away.

Mum's IPF had been fast-moving and degenerative. The disease causes scarring in the lung tissue and, though otherwise healthy, she struggled to breathe. Still she tried to be the active person she had been, playing with her grandchildren and going on walks, but as the disease took hold her skin paled, her nails curved and the lines in her face became etched and deep. I remember a family weekend in Bournemouth where she was forever stopping to gasp for air. On one short walk up a hill her lips went blue. Watching her fight for breath broke my heart.

Initially, I remained very matter-of-fact. My responsibility as the eldest son was to support my parents, my brother and my sister by thinking and acting positively and not dwelling on the negatives. I went to all the appointments and researched as much about IPF as I could. Mum and I were made of the same stuff in this respect: let's find a solution to this problem and fight hard.

But when it became clear that the end was near, the regime unravelled. The week following her death was a blur. It was then that I finally cried. I had so much admiration for her. Throughout all her suffering Mum had always acted with grace. Standing up in church and reading the eulogy was one of the toughest things I have ever done.

So, before commencing the climb today I had taken a moment to gather my thoughts, knowing that this was a day I would never forget. I was about to cycle up the famous Tourmalet, and I was doing it for Nicola, for the boys, and for my mother. For the second time in two days I had a lump in my throat.

'Miss you, Mum,' I whispered to the distant summit.

It was in the 1910 Tour de France that the Tourmalet was introduced, the first time the *Grand Bouclé* had traversed a peak more than 2000 metres high. The riders had hated it. The dirt track was wholly unsuitable for cycling, the gradients far beyond what their single speed bicycles could manage, and many cursed Henri Desgrange, the Tour founder. It had actually been Desgrange's right hand man, Alphonse Steinès, who had conducted the reconnaissance, and despite having been prevented from reaching the summit on the terrible road owing to snow, despite having fallen in a stream and nearly frozen to death, he had sent a telegram to Desgrange: 'Tourmalet crossed. Stop. Very good road. Stop. Perfectly acceptable. Stop.' Had he wanted the riders to suffer? Desgrange once declared that his ideal tour would be one in which 'only one rider survived the ordeal.' It's becoming very clear what he meant as we inch our way upwards.

With a third of the climb done, the incline goes from steady to steep and the weather worsens, the rain now falling as snow and accumulating on the verge in thick lines of greying sludge. JB is no longer singing. We are soaked through and freezing, noses red raw from the icy wind, fingers and toes in that painful, prickly state of having been numb for hours. Upwards we ride through the car park of the ski resort. This time, snow paints the slopes, but with the chair lifts stationary there is a somewhat eerie atmosphere.

Peter has parked in a lay-by and we pause. 'I'll check how much snow is on the summit,' he says, and disappears off up the road. The temperature has dropped noticeably.

'Damn it!' says Nobby as he and Mark join us. 'I was hoping to grab my gloves from Pete.' The next two kilometres seem endless until the van reappears with the gloves.

'It's bad,' says Peter. 'Three to four inches. You might have to walk the last kilometre.'

'How are we all feeling about this?' I ask.

Graham: 'Fine. We'll walk if we have to.'

'Bugger that,' says Ben, 'I'll ride it.'

'Yep. I'm up for riding,' says JB.

'Are we sure?' Allen is more cautious.

'Let's keep going,' says Mark. Simon and Nobby nod in agreement.

'Careful then, fellas.' Peter climbs back in the driver's seat and shuts the door against the biting wind. Jealously, we return to our saddles.

Onwards we ride, meeting another herd being brought down from the snow-laden upper slopes. Suddenly it makes sense: this is no place for animals. No place for cyclists either, but up we go. Icy breaths fill lungs, all extremities without feeling, the sweat generated by the constant effort cooling to a body-shaking damp. The roar of a snow plough grows audibly from behind, but there's no caution, no apparent acknowledgement of the blizzard from the driver, and the vehicle hurtles past, an inch from clipping Mark, making him wobble out of control towards the edge, which does nothing to help his vertigo.

The temperature hovers around the freezing mark on the final approach to the summit, the road steeper now as it reaches its highest point, snow covering everything, the air itself a white-grey. Tyres carefully follow the ploughed channel as flakes flutter in faces. Shouts of 'Crazy!' escape from car windows, the few drivers also making the pass astonished at these cyclists, *les fous*, the madmen.

A turn in the road reveals the larger-than-life figure of *Le Géant du Tourmalet*, the monument that commemorates Octave Lapize having been the first to reach the summit on that Tour in 1910. He had walked much of the way, cursing the race officials as he struggled: *'Vous êtes des assassins!'* The grey metal of the statue lies beneath a layer of white that part-masks the cyclist's pain-contorted face. We have pictured it many times before. In no one's imagination had there been snow.

'Did you see that plough?' Ben and Allen are gasping as they reach the statue. 'That madman driver nearly killed us! Ben almost fell off the mountain to get out of the way. Thank god no one else was coming.'

Cheers and applause come from others who have made the climb in more appropriate vehicles; we are all utterly frozen and overwhelmed after such an intense climb and emotions are running high. Ben is practically dancing to stay warm; the heavy slush on the verge has found its way up through his summer shoes. I shelter behind the van to call Nicola, but most of what she can hear is the biting wind and my teeth chattering. We feel every bit the *fous*, the first cyclists to reach the summit today, and the first in the snow this season. We are overcome with relief, exhaustion and triumph. The mountain has not won.

It was less than a year ago that our fledgling team took part in its first proper sportive: *Ay Up! Yorkshire*, a looping ride through the North York Moors. The purpose was to kick-start some hill training and boy, did it provide. For 93 miles (and the shorter option of 56 miles for me) we struggled through the unrelenting landscape, with good old Yorkshire gradients of 25%, and while the scenery was gorgeous, the effort was immense. A baptism of fire, you might say. Most of us had never even cycled 50 miles before. But we had a blast that day, which was only a sign of things to come. Looking back on our motley crew, it's amazing to think how much we've progressed.

Among our team that day was Stuart Eadie. A good friend of mine, Stuey was one of the original eight – in fact, the first person I asked to be part of the team. We'd been on one or two snowboarding holidays together so I knew he'd be up for the challenge, though our preferred type of physical activity usually involved a few too many beers on Après-Ski afternoons. One Saturday, after plying him with booze, I'd mentioned the challenge, going on about iconic Tour peaks (only naming three), beautiful weather and stunning scenery. It wasn't until the hangover subsided and he'd already agreed that I revealed the full extent of the plan. Nevertheless, he was there at each early morning ride, each weekend meander, receiving his fair share of Peaky grief as we continually ripped him for being the shortest of the bunch. At every meeting we would pull out a high chair for him; often we'd turn up to training with a kid's tricycle or a step ladder for his bike. Not long into the process his wife fell pregnant. Stuey's training rides began to take a back seat.

Already it feels as though we've suffered enough, but the Tourmalet is just peak one of the day's three. The descent begins, a cautious freewheel in the ploughed tracks, but the erratic plough driver hasn't done quite as thorough a job on this side and patches of sludge slide the tarmac from beneath our tyres. Falling on day two is not a risk I would like to take so I hop in the van along with Mark, Nobby, Graham and Allen, and we huddle in close proximity for a couple of kilometres. Out of the white-out landscape we emerge onto the frozen slopes once more, the snow melting to rain in the lower altitude. Hands grow numb long before we reach the bottom, fingers clutching painfully at brakes. Ben and Simon declined the lift, neither of them willing to pass on an inch of the downhill, and JB is in tow to make sure they make it in one piece.

At our lunch stop we make a rendezvous with a good friend from Wantage, Paul Mead, who made the move out here more than ten years ago. He addresses the café owner in perfect Franglais.

'Makes a change from your Del Boy impression, Macca,' says Ben.

'What are you all having?' he asks us. 'There's baguettes, baguettes or baguettes.'

The food is something of a problem. I don't usually eat bread, but there's precious little choice. It's worse for Nobby, the vegetarian among us. In France, meat is considered a flavouring. His baguette returns, looking very anaemic, with a sprinkling of cheese inside the pale bread. We shove them down – appetising or not, it's food, and we need all the fuel we can get.

While finishing off chewing, Paul comes over and shakes my hand. 'I have to hand it to you,' he says. 'I've been over these passes many times, and it's tough enough driving, never mind being on a bike. Even my neighbours who have lived here their whole lives find the mountains daunting. There's a kind of reverence that surrounds them.' Since the beginning Paul had been in awe of what we were doing. A keen rider himself, he's cycled the nearby Col d'Aspin, but said he would never climb the Tourmalet – to him, it was simply a climb too far. 'You've done it. That's seriously impressive. You're pretty much unstoppable once you've set your mind to something. And in this weather! Phew. Well done.'

The meandering Adour de Payolle river tracks the road through the valley until we begin our ascent of the next pass, the Col d'Aspin. Thick pines line the road, the views back down the valley masked with low-hanging cloud. The lower slopes are once more awash with rain, a persistent biting at our faces that eventually puts paid to even Simon's smile. We are soon soaked to the skin. The road kicks upwards for the final 5km, a winding ascent in the coniferous forest, and as we emerge from the trees onto the summit pasture, in a glorious moment, the rain finally eases and the sun comes out.

Ben is doing a terrific job. His smile has never waned, and he's always going for a hug with whoever is closest. Some of the team have more than a decade on him so Ben is definitely the kid of the bunch, though in all honesty there's not much maturity in the rest of us. I first met Ben through our local cycling club Grench, though with him being a pretty zippy cyclist, our interactions were only ever a brief greeting as he headed off in the A team while I settled in with team B. Cycling had been an escape for Ben. Having spent most of his working life by the seaside, moving to central Oxfordshire didn't provide much opportunity for yacht maintenance or kayak coaching. His first road bike cost £35 and was a few sizes too small, but soon Ben was drawn into the club culture and found that cycling really suited him. The tallest and largest of the lads, at first glance Ben might not appear to be the type to climb many mountains, but he was one of the first to sign up for the Peaky Climbers. Perhaps he was attracted by all the downhills.

His girlfriend Catherine thought the challenge was just another of his lofty ideas; Ben's a dreamer, always going on about sailing around the world. But it became clear that this was serious. It would require a proper kick-start in terms of fitness: at 17st 7lb, Ben was carrying a lot of weight. Time to get in shape.

Though our adventure is less than 48 hours old, it already seems an age ago that we sat on the plane making the journey here. The flight was full of optimism, excitement and a healthy dose of trepidation, the kind a rock band might feel before stepping out on stage. Rehearsals done, all that is left to do is ride, though in truth, the nerves were less about the challenge and more about our kit. There was almost a competition, as we manhandled our bike boxes to the check-in, about how much over the weight limit we were. The boxes were processed one by one, and we glanced sideways at each other as each passed without comment, despite our having stuffed them as full as we possibly could, with a week's worth of food shoved alongside gloves, shoes and our precious Peaky Climbers jerseys.

'See you on the other side, bikey,' said Nobby as the boxes passed into the void.

'Let's hope they don't bloody lose them,' said Simon.

The Col de Peyresourde concludes our ride today, a day typified by terrible weather, stoic attitudes and a determination to keep going through it all. The long, steady climb rises through corn fields and empty villages, weaving between fields of cattle, the shelter growing thinner as the ascent gains height, pain and determination etched into our faces. This is without doubt the toughest thing any of us has ever encountered. We were naïve, failing to imagine how terrible the weather might be, even though the forecasts were for searing heat. But now we appreciate how unpredictable riding in the mountains can be. Though we've cycled in rain before, it's been nothing like this.

The vegetation grows sparse near the peak, rough brushstrokes of browns and greens with pine trees darkening the slopes in patches. The road levels off to where the signpost stands, marking the highest point of the pass. The relief is palpable; there will be no more climbing today. And that's it, an exhausted snake down, a team of yellow bugs freewheeling around the corners on graffiti-strewn roads. Soon we will reach the hotel, where the comfort of the evening routine will take over: unload the vans, shower, stretch, pile into the dining room for yet another feast. We'll settle down for a beer (wine for Graham) and do our best to recover. It's my job to crack the whip, to make sure the guys are keeping on top of it all – 'Right,

Peaky Climbers...' has already become a catch phrase. We could all do well to take a leaf out of JB's book: Mr Organised, he lays out his kit and fills his water bottles the night before, then leaps up in the morning, no time to waste.

As the descent spirals us back to ground level the sun returns, bouncing in blinding reflections from the tarmac, and we are finally able to lift our heads and appreciate the beauty of our surroundings. The snow of this morning seems like a distant memory. What a day.

Day Three

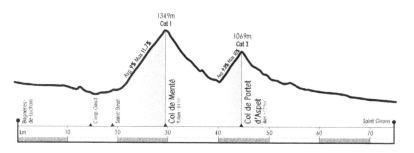

One of the steepest climbs of the Pyrenees, Col de Menté was the slope on which Luis Ocaña saw his dreams of winning the 1971 Tour slip away. The Spaniard had fought hard to gain an advantage over Merckx, day after day fending off the Belgian, eventually clocking up an incredible seven minute lead on his rival. But on the descent of the Col de Menté, Merckx attacked, charging down his prey on roads slick with rain. Overtaken and seeing his hard-won advantage slipping away, Ocaña gave chase. But his skill in downhill couldn't match the Cannibal's, especially in such weather. Even though Merckx crashed to the ground on a slippery corner, he picked himself up and threw himself back down the mountain, a descent that would eventually gift him the stage and the Tour. Ocaña slipped on the very same corner, but unlike Merckx he did not get up again. His race ended in a hospital bed, Merckx's on the podium, the third of his five tour wins.

We're chancing it with the weather – it's lovely and mild, and most of us roll out optimistically in our summer layers. Erring on the side of caution, Sensible Allen and JB have dressed properly, and smile ironically at the rest of us as the rain begins its inevitable fall.

The miles pass easily as we make our way towards the Col de Menté, a gentle downhill giving our legs a chance to loosen up before the day's climbing begins. But I don't feel right, and shortly into the ride I pull over and throw up. Well, that was a waste of a nearly-good breakfast and much-needed calories. I wasn't able to keep my dinner down last night, either. Maybe it's the dodgy food, but it's more likely to be the exertion – our bodies are being put through a hell of a lot. Mark had similar issues on some of our training rides. I try to take on food but after the contents of my stomach end up on the verge a second time I just say, 'sod it' and head up the climb with the lads.

'Are you OK?' Allen asks. 'I can check the first aid kit for some Pepto-bismol if you like.'

'Thanks, but I'm sure it will pass.'

'Good old Allen,' says Ben. 'A true Boy Scout. Always prepared!'

Allen, the Scout Leader and all-round outdoors man, has

proven invaluable in our training rides, the designated puncture fixer, the voice of reason when we want to go too far and too fast, and the one who patches us up when we take a tumble.

I'm dizzy by the time we reach the summit, though thankfully the sickness has passed and I manage to nibble an energy bar. Food is not just fuel, it's morale. I could really do with some of Nicola's flapjacks right now – she made so many during our training that they became my lucky charm. Soaked, cold and desperate for a coffee, we herd into the summit café to drip onto the floor.

It took three weeks for Allen to come on board. Full of admiration for the guys who had signed up, at no point did he think he'd be one of them. A considered man is our Allen, not frivolous or careless; it's almost no surprise that he works as an accountant. He's my polar opposite. Understated and timid, he is not one for profanity, whereas he says I can't complete a sentence without swearing. He's the type to sit quietly at the side while I'm in the centre of it all. But a team cannot be full of alpha males – we needed someone like Allen. And he's a really solid cyclist. His small stature belies his strength: the pocket rocket we call him, with calves that could out-do most people's thighs.

Grench rides were at that point dominated by talk

of training plans, and Allen would quietly listen to our conversations, wanting no more than to support the lads with their preparation. 'I've looked at the route of your challenge,' he said one day. 'Well, I started looking but it was so ridiculous I gave up.' So his eventual agreement came completely out of the blue. While relaxing in the pub after a ride one Sunday, he turned to me. 'I think your challenge is absolutely mad. Usually I would say it's the kind of thing other people do. But I think it's time to be one of those people.'

The making of a team is 70% luck and 30% judgement. From the outset, my mind was set on the magic number of eight. Like Noah's Ark, we could go up two by two, or in fours, or all together. Odd numbers just didn't make sense. All the planning had been done with eight riders in mind, so with six people signed up I was after a couple more.

It had been a few months since I'd first mentioned the ride to JB, and I'd been badgering him about it ever since. One of my skiing buddies, I was confident he'd be at home in the mountains. Another challenge was preventing him from committing, but once the plans for that fell through, it was time to try again. I picked up the phone.

'Yes, Macca.'

'I've heard your LEJOG has been postponed.'

'I was trying to keep that quiet!'

'You know what I'm going to say...'

'OK. Okay, okay, I'll do it. Just let me ask Mandy.'

After much eye-rolling, she agreed.

The Col de Portet d'Aspet is only half the length of the Col de Menté, but with a 10% average gradient and a 14% slope to begin, it is a kick. Pairings assumed, jackets removed, we commence the climb. The road is thick with trees and beneath a low-slung canopy we ride, through a tunnel of vibrant green, where rain water grasps at leaves and a fine mist hovers between the branches. It feels as though we are in the middle of a rain forest. The familiar psychological battle with the slope begins, counting down to each hairpin, talking through the pedal strokes, knowing that to stop pushing will only make it harder. We delude ourselves that the gradient will level off around the next corner, but of course it doesn't. Higher and higher we ascend, hearts racing and legs straining. It's tough, and cold. Why won't it stop bloody raining? In the midst of a climb, lost in the struggle of it all, it's easy to lose focus. I think of Nicola back in Wantage, comfortable and warm. She will be at work right now, probably on a sales call, and will take our dog out for a walk afterwards. Every evening I give her the lowdown and let her know we are still alive, and ask after the boys. How welcoming the mundane seems in the midst of our suffering. In this moment, I get a sharp stab of missing her, and feel more than ever an appreciation of what she has put up with this year. While I've been off pursuing my dreams Nicola has held everything else together, running the home and caring for the children, sorting out Jai's imminent departure to university, all the while churning out those flapjacks. It hasn't always been smooth, and we've had our fair share of tiffs, but I could never have completed this without her full support. I look around at the others and know it's the same for them.

The rain continues its slow soak. Whatever we do, we have these moments of doubt, the moments when we question our motivations. Did we really put our partners through all that for this? But I have always been a doer, never able to sit still for long, always planning the next big thing. For this is how we develop as people. In all the training, all the hills climbed to get to this point, each muscle-ripping incline, each expletive uttered, each late-night, rain-washed, mud-splattered training ride there is satisfaction. It is in doing things that we grow. Experiences make us who we are, and we want to reach the end of our lives not regretful of what we didn't do, but feeling proud of what we did.

Part way up the climb is the monument to the Italian rider Fabio Casartelli, a marble sculpture of a bicycle wheel standing on a plinth a short way back from the road. It was in the 1995 Tour de France that Casartelli crashed on this descent, fatally smashing his head as he fell. We stop to pay our respects in turn as we pass, as the Tour riders always do. A chiselled cloth flows out from the wheel as if in continuous motion, a sign of Fabio forever riding, and on the marble below, there is a drilled hole through which the sun shines every 18th July, the date of his death, at noon. Would a helmet have prevented his premature death? The racing scene has changed so much in the past two decades, the professional peloton now cocooned in protective headgear and sunglasses, items that are more science than sports-based, contributing to speed with their aerodynamic design. It's a different world from the time of Fausto Coppi and Eddy Merckx, with their solid steel bicycles, unprotected eyes, and at most, the team cycling cap perched on their head. There were protests when helmets were made compulsory and for the first couple of years, riders were allowed to ditch their lids on the last climb of the day if the finish was at the summit, resulting in a curious ritual of polystyrene tops being hurled to the verge.

The tree cover thins on the final stretch and we crest the brow onto the wide open summit, greeted by the gusting wind and, thankfully, the two support vans. The seating arrangements are not the most spacious so we take it in turns to hop in, shivering, attempting to dry out, removing soaking wet gloves to reveal crocodile hands and numb fingers. The mandatory summit photo is taken, then we pile back on to the bikes and begin the descent. It is a long 30km ride to our stop, and with conversation muted by the downpour and clothes saturated, we are desperate for lunch.

In the warmth, with chatter and clatter of plates, easy conversation and laughter, the hardship begins to fade. Condensation clouds the windows as the day's troubles gently evaporate.

Organising the Peaky Climbers' training regime was delegated to Mark. As a founding member of Grench we assumed he knew what he was doing, though he would be the first to admit he made it up as he went along. Grench was formed as a social cycling club, a chance to do some easy riding with a group of mates. Once a week there would be a 30 mile spin, nothing too arduous, with a pint stop halfway and another at the Fox in Denchworth to finish. To become Kings of the Mountains we would have to be far more serious.

Mark was terrific at getting the team regimented. Here we were, eight guys who were carrying a bit of weight, trying to get fit enough to attempt what the pros do in the Tour de France. We rode out every weekend, whoever could make it, steadily increasing the mileage and the difficulty, with three or four additional sessions during the week. At first the tactic was to climb as many hills as possible, but after spending five miserable hours trudging up and down Sincombe Hill, the total elevation of which was less than we'd be facing on day one, we realised there were better ways to go about it. We simply needed to get out there and, in the words of Eddy Merckx, *Ride lots*. We did fast rides, long rides, short, steep hills rides, long drags and multi-day excursions. There were monthly gym sessions to build our core strength and stability, trying to find that elusive six-pack where, predictably, we would attempt to beat each other on reps, with Mark and Nobby usually taking it to extremes. JB would map our rides, analysing the distance and elevation and often adding a database of the pubs en-route – he had a spreadsheet for everything. The Fox became our unofficial headquarters, the venue of our fortnightly meetings and the scene of many a rowdy post-ride gathering – with the exception of Allen, we kept going with the beers.

Training filtered into every part of our lives. JB took his bike to his brother's wedding to fit in a ride before the ceremony. Allen cycled home from a family holiday to Dorset, a 100 mile ride, while his wife Kirstie and their son followed in the car the next day. After a mate's 50th birthday party in Milton Keynes, I rose at 7.30am to ride the 60 miles home. Most of us went out on Christmas Day, Boxing Day, New Year and birthdays. Our partners thought we were mad.

Soon after our *Ay Up!* sportive we were on our way to Wales for the day, for a change of scenery and a challenge greater than the local Uffington hills. After an early morning drive along a windswept and rainy M4 we pulled up near the Monmouthshire town of Usk, near the confluence of the Brecon Beacons and Black Mountains, to arrive at our luxury changing facilities, a lay-by near a disused pub. The plan was to ride the Tumble, a pass near Abergavenny, famous for being one of the toughest climbs in Wales. For six kilometres it rises at an average gradient of 8.3%, topping out at 15% near the start, and sustaining double figures for much of the climb. It was a fraction of what we'd be facing in the Alps but it would be the longest continuous climb any of us had yet attempted.

Full of optimism and jokes about the shocking weather, we set off from our newly-dubbed Wales Training Base, and spun into the countryside. It soon became clear we had totally underestimated the ride. With wind, rain and an unfamiliar route, we were soon far behind schedule. Ben slipped and slashed his calf and the Garmins ran out of juice. Route-less, hungry and freezing cold we stopped in a café, eating so much and taking so long we had to miss out the Tumble.

By December another Wales trip was on the cards, the first time that all eight Peaky Climbers had coordinated a training ride together, and this time we were determined to take on the famous climb. Once again, we headed to our training base, the luxurious Lay-by de Pub, and with an earlier start time and pockets full of snacks we hit the Tumble. This was one of our milestones, the markers by which we measured our progress; with eight different lives and routines to work around, there was no chance we would all make every training ride each time. The milestones were our focus, our key rides, the sessions for which we would make that extra effort. It was a gruelling, windy and difficult ride, and for Ben in particular, a struggle. He would never have made it if it weren't for Allen, who stuck by his side and encouraged him up the climb. It had taken a while for Allen to fit into the team – never having had a group of male friends like it, he was nervous at first to be in amongst all the loud-mouths. But supporting others was where he came into his own. He would never let anyone struggle, and as he shared this natural caring side with the team, his confidence grew.

Winter was a difficult time. There had already been five solid months of hard work, the initial buzz of training had waned, the days were short, cold and wet, and there were still months and months to go. Each of us was approaching the challenge with our own tactics, but it had become clear to the team that Ben was struggling. There had been much talk of power-to-weight ratio that 'proper' cyclists focus on, that physical size out-balances power output once the inclines kick in, and though Ben's strength was impressive, his weight was substantial. 'Just hit the road hard,' Mark would say in our Fox hangouts, his own training regime to cycle 20 miles as fast as he could, eventually getting it down to under an hour. 'That's all you need to do. Works for me.' While Allen and Nobby were cycling the 30 miles home from work, Ben's commute was only two. JB and Simon would set up the turbo trainer at home for an evening of pedalling in front of the TV. Nobby was a devotee of spinning, and Mark would constantly rib him for it. By listening to seven differing sets of advice, Ben wasn't making much progress.

'Perhaps it's time to get a proper training plan together,' JB said after a particularly depressing and rainy session. 'Copying the rest of us probably isn't going to cut it for you. Give my cycling coach a call – I'm sure he'll help.'

Simon completed the eight. His wife, another Nicky, came from Denchworth, so he often found himself in the Fox, and at his father-in-law's funeral Simon bonded with Mark, which is always dangerous. Before we knew it, Simon was attending the weekly Grench rides and rediscovering his love for cycling. So when the King of the Mountains challenge was mentioned, it piqued Simon's interest. Though social rides and touring were more his thing, the buzz of a challenge, the sense of achievement in pursuing a goal, the camaraderie and team spirit were almost too tempting to resist. But he had been so long out of the saddle. Would it be possible to climb all those mountains with the excess bulk?

'You should go for it,' Nicky said when he mentioned it. 'The chance to do something like this doesn't come along very often. It's great to see you back on your bike, and this sounds like an amazing challenge. Totally crazy, but amazing.'

'But what about the pub? And what about you?'

'Look, we live in each other's pockets as it is. It might do us some good for you to have a project that doesn't involve work or me. I don't want you to look back on this moment in ten years' time and regret not taking part.'

So Simon said yes, and was the perfect piece to complete the Peaky Climbers jigsaw. A kind, warm-hearted guy who everyone loves, who provided balance alongside the chest-beaters. We came to adore that smile of his.

As well as the British Lung Foundation, we are raising money for the Caring Cancer Trust, a charity that runs activity weekends to help children regain their self-confidence and re-ignite their passion for life after the trauma caused by their illness and treatment. Everyone is affected by cancer in one way or another. Allen lost his mother-in-law to the disease, Ben his godfather, and in 2015 local girl Maisie Norton lost her seven-year battle with cancer.

Maisie's death rocked the town of Wantage. Well-known in our small community, she was a personal friend of ours, similar in age to Jai and to Nobby's son Sam, good friends with JB's daughter Charlotte, and especially close to Allen and Kirstie, who had known her before her diagnosis and along the roller coaster of good news followed by bad. Throughout her illness, her positive attitude, infectious laugh and cheeky personality never failed. An overflowing church on the day of her funeral was testament to how many people's lives were touched by Maisie. As Allen said, you couldn't know her and not like her.

Maisie had twice been on activity holidays run by the Caring Cancer Trust, trips that, in her own words, changed her perspective on life. It was a rare chance to be a normal teenager and share experiences with others who had been through similar challenges. So she devoted much of her time to raising funds and awareness of the charity, and mentoring other children going through the same. In her honour the charity placed her favourite flower, the Pink Gerbera, on their logo.

It was Nobby's suggestion to raise funds for the Caring Cancer Trust in memory of Maisie, and the team immediately agreed. It would transform the project into something in which we all had an emotional stake. Raising money for Maisie felt like the right thing to do.

By May we had smashed our fundraising goal of £30,000.

£30k in six months! The support we received was mind-blowing. That initial figure had seemed too huge, far beyond what anyone really thought was possible. But that was my vision and I wholeheartedly believed we could make it happen. With a calendar of events together with individual targets of £4,000, our charity pot slowly grew, a chipping away of the total, in the same steady way that one climbs a hill. A 'Yes' man by nature, having already worn the guys down to join the team in the first place (they might say bullying, I would say persuasive), I pushed them to achieve. Yes, we can raise the money, yes, we can climb these mountains, yes, we can do this.

Things kicked off with an Après-Ski party in January, a homage to the legendary post-ski drinks that take place on the slopes. We would transport the Austrian Alps to Wantage with fake snow, ski lifts, Rodeo Reindeer and glühwein in a massive decorated marquee. The aim was not only to raise the roof but some serious money. Tickets were £25 and with a capacity of 350 we had some work to do; the guys didn't for one minute believe we would sell 200 tickets, let alone 350. But I was convinced. It was like any of our training trips; they were a test to see where our capabilities lay, and this was no different. To fit it all in on top of everything else we were already doing was a challenge, to say the least. But the community rallied around, and with a marquee donated by Ben's company, and a DJ, lighting company, drinks van and carpenter helping out for free, it ended up being the party of the year. We sold all those tickets. Guests wore bobble hats, scarves, ski boots and goggles, and with Mark in charge of our fancy dress, the Peaky team appeared in Bavarian barmaid outfits complete with stockings, mini-skirts, basques and long blond plaited wigs. Eight grown men bursting out of our corsets – we looked ridiculous. Danny la Rue springs to mind, though with far less elegance and fewer sequins. We served ski shots from the tables, preserving our dignity with Peaky Climbers branded boxer shorts. Reps from the charities came, and when Maisie's dad stood up to deliver a personal and moving speech, 350 people stood and listened. The charities said they had never seen anything like it. More than £12,500 was raised in just that one night.

And that was the kick-start we needed. If we could pull that off, imagine how far we could go. With five figures in the bank we forged onwards full tilt, with a Pimm's party, prosecco party, golf day, Denchfest and a gig with Nobby's band. The donations crept up. Nearing the challenge we undertook a Spinathon – spin-fan Nobby's idea – though after doing back-to-back spin classes for seven hours, with sore bums, numb minds and aching legs, we had only raised £300. 'I'm never speaking to Nobby again!' said Mark afterwards. 'I would gladly have paid that to not do it!'

It was always a priority that not one penny of the donations would be used to fund the trip itself, so we needed corporate sponsors to cover our costs. And this was where I came into my own, bringing local businesses on board. 'Paul could sell snow to the Eskimos,' the others would say. I just knew that with the team, the challenge and the charities we were on to a good thing – all that was needed was for others to buy into my vision and see we were not just a bunch of tin pot cyclists after some free kit.

Approaching two good friends was the first step. Clive Robson, director of local property developer Bellwood projects, and Steve Aram, manager of vehicle security firm VTech systems, had both considered being on the team itself, but financial support made more sense for them. Being close to Maisie and the Norton family, Clive threw himself into helping the cause; it was he who worked so hard to stage the Après-Ski party along with his party-planning partner Nicky Henshall. Clive and Steve had both played football for me in Milton Utd Veterans, so they were well aware I could start a project from scratch and make it fly. It took a couple of meetings of Dragons' Den style pitching for them to verbally agree. Then when it came to signing on the dotted line I upped their commitments.

'Er, Macca, this says slightly more than you told us last week.'

'Oh, does it? Sorry, pen must have slipped. You're alright with that though, aren't you…?'

They knew me too well to take offence. Laughing, we got our signatures.

With two headline companies secured, there followed a couple of months of trailing around with my laptop, showing my presentation and gradually selling all the sponsorship spots. Eventually I had a full suite of corporate sponsors and enough funds in the bank to pay the deposit to Le Domestique. That was a good day. We were now fully committed – there was no turning back.

With seven peaks climbed in three days, that is it for the Pyrenees. Ahead is a five hour transfer to Provence; with eight full-grown men squashed into two vans, there's precious little space to stretch our aching legs and no escape from whoever keeps breaking wind. We pull up for a pit stop, and there is the Team Sky bus, parked at the service station.

'Look who it is!'

'They must have heard the Peaky Climbers were in town.'

We disembark and walk over to their coach, our transport looking ridiculous in comparison. Inside, the seating is spacious and the upholstery comfortable. Printed on the side is the team list with the names of each of their riders.

'We should've done that on ours!' says Ben.

'Looks like the pros don't have to put up with school minibus conditions,' says Simon.

'Where are they?' The service station is quiet, with no sign of the team.

'Damn; it would have been incredible to meet them!'

'They must be gutted they missed us!'

The journey resumes and we sing along as JB and Ben practice their dad-dancing. But beneath the easy laughter lurks an underlying tension, the thought that tomorrow comes Mont Ventoux: the most notorious of all the climbs and the one that each of us has been fearing the most. It was discussed or at least mentioned at virtually every team meeting. The challenge is to climb it not just once, but to attempt all three of the mountain's ascents in a single day: once from Bédoin, once from Malaucène, and the third from Sault. Few cyclists even attempt this, never mind complete it. The vans speed along the motorway, the Pyrenees left far behind as Ventoux's brutish bulk rises across the plain. And on glimpsing the peak, all conversation falls silent.

Day Four

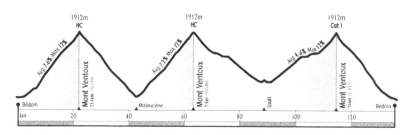

Ventoux. The name itself puts fear in the heart, not scared fear, but a kind of reverence and respect, the kind of fear you might have for God. Because this is what the Ventoux is: a god. A god of evil, some say, to whom sacrifices must be made. And Ventoux would certainly take sacrifices. Its slopes have humbled many a cyclist, amateur and pro; even the great Eddy Merckx needed oxygen after his 1970 ascent. Its unforgiving gradient pushes riders to the absolute limit. Most tragically, it claimed the life of Tom Simpson, the British cyclist who collapsed a kilometre or so from the summit in 1967. He was one of those rare Brits who had made a name for himself on the continent: the first to wear the yellow jersey, and world champion in 1965. But the arid mountain slopes on that overwhelmingly hot day proved too much for him. He lost consciousness, a cocktail of alcohol and amphetamines in his stomach.

The mountain dominates the landscape, the infamous slopes visible from miles around, seeming all the more daunting for being isolated from any range. Thick forest cloaks its lower half and its bald head shines as if with snow. The tower of the observatory rises skyward from the peak, giving it the aura of a science experiment. Such is the power of Ventoux that it affects weather as well as cyclists.

It's Simon's wedding anniversary. Twenty five years ago today he married Nicky.

'Nice hair!' says JB as we pass around the wedding photos at breakfast. 'Shall we call you Simon le Bon from now on?'

Simon smiles and generally ignores us as he opens Nicky's card, then fends us off as we bundle him with kisses and hugs.

'So how are you feeling being miles away from your good lady wife?' I ask.

'Honestly, this anniversary is the reason I almost didn't join the team,' Simon replies. 'I didn't want to spend it apart from Nicky.'

'I guess she didn't mind seeing the back of you, though,' says JB.

Simon laughs. 'Actually, she is the one who encouraged me. She told me not to worry about the anniversary. This would be a once-in-a-lifetime chance to be part of something with a group of new friends. And it has been, for her as well as for me.'

'Bet she's regretting it now she knows how much dollar you spent upgrading your bike,' says Nobby with a wink.

The next cards to be handed around are the 'Cinglés Club' cards, the papers that will be stamped to prove we have completed all three of Ventoux's ascents; these will become cherished parts of our cycling memorabilia. *Cinglé*. French for crazy. Off one's head. We're going to become the Loons of Ventoux. Happy anniversary Simon.

The ascent from Bédoin in the south, the most frequently used in the Tour de France, will elevate us more than 1200m to reach the ski station at Le Chalet Reynard, then a further 500m to the peak. From there we will descend the western slope to Malaucène, about-turn, and climb up again. Descending the southern side again as if to Bédoin, we will fork left at Le Chalet Reynard for Sault, from where we will climb back up for the final time. Silence replaces the usual banter about which climb of the day will be the hardest. All bets are off: we know full well that each will be as tough as the next.

Ascent one: Bédoin. We roll out of the village towards the giant. There's no gentle incline, no preparation for the climb. As soon as we're out of the plains and into the forest the road ramps steeply, the gradient as good as doubling in a single pedal stroke.

Mark and Nobby head the pack as usual, and soon disappear around the corner.

'Good luck, fellas. See you at the top,' Simon calls after them.

'There must be something going on between those two,' says Graham.

'The two Janes certainly think so!' says Ben.

We joke for a while about Nobby and Mark's bromance – they are joined at the hip, always saving a seat for each other at dinner, sharing a room, riding next to each other, training together. We've nicknamed them Hinge and Bracket after the old drag act of the 70s, and their affection for each other is a constant source of team banter, though I reckon we're all secretly jealous.

Allen and Ben soon slide away up the slope, and with Graham and Simon settling in behind, JB and I launch our assault, our legs a steady metronome marking our plodding progress up the mountain. The gradient bites with each stroke, the effort felt in each muscle, each sinew, each brain cell. It's dry for a change, and the sun filtering through the leaves casts patches of gold and green on the road. The forest, thick with pine, leaches a delicious aroma into the clear air, and the tree cover encloses us in a tunnel. No wonder this mountain holds such wonder, such reverence, such fame. No one who has ever been here would forget it.

'Climbing Ventoux three times is the equivalent to all the climbs we did yesterday and the day before combined,' says JB.

That's not quite what I wanted to hear, but JB has proven to be a priceless member of the team, and I'm so glad the stars aligned to enable him to join. His obsession with detail and planning, and the way he analyses the minutiae of everything we are doing, is a source of constant teasing from everyone on the team – as well as being bloody useful. Even though it took a while to persuade him to take part, once signed up he threw himself head-first into the project. He's a steadfast guy, the type who would give you his last fiver to make sure you survived.

'How's your back holding up?' I ask.

'A few niggles but nothing major. So far, so good.' It was back trouble that brought JB to cycling in the first place, after he'd had to give up his beloved cricket after 30 years of regular playing.

'Do you miss it?' I ask.

'Yes and no. I'll always love cricket but there are plenty of similarities with cycling. Just being part of a team is great, whatever the sport, and you guys enjoy a beer and a cake as much as the cricket lads. And of course banter and cricket go hand in hand – you should hear the comments at the crease!' We nod to a couple of riders as they slip easily past us. 'Honestly, I never thought I'd be a cyclist, but with Grench and now this – I'm proud that I can call myself one.'

Another team overtakes, working hard against the gradient. Ventoux is the most popular mountain we've climbed so far. Soon we are the ones to overtake a group who are locked in battle with the slope. Someone on an e-bike zips past, waving cheerily. At Le Chalet Reynard we see him again, sitting on the verge, chirpiness gone.

'Everything alright, mate?'

'Battery's out,' he replies.

It's a curious thing, pain. Thoughts swing wildly between wanting the whole bloody thing to be over, and wishing that the adventure would last forever. Simon calls these the goldfish moments. One minute we are cursing the sheer ridiculousness of it all, overwhelmed with the effort, the discomfort and the pain, then we forget our suffering and spend the following hour feeling invincible, chatting about what we might take on next. At various times we've all hit those walls, when we've felt at the absolute end of our physical and mental capabilities, then out of nowhere comes a spark that allows you to smash on through.

Emerging from the forest, there is a sudden shift in the landscape. The luscious green is replaced by a blinding wilderness of limestone scree which extends loosely in every direction. The whole scene is reminiscent of the slag heaps in mining towns, though in a photographic negative. Boulders shine in the sun's glare and exposed rock faces glow where the road cuts through them, revealing white stones, the like of which none of us has ever seen. It feels as though we are cycling on the moon.

JB had warned us about how unpredictable the weather can be up here, that in the height of summer the sun blasts the arid slopes, and in winter full blizzards can whip around the peak while the town of Bédoin sits peacefully below. Today, we are met by wind, which howls and rips across our path. The tree line fades into the distance as the road climbs ever higher, and with no shelter the gusts increase in ferocity. No longer gently curving, the road is now a zigzag of switchbacks, the wind slapping in our faces at each turn, practically stopping us in our tracks. There's no option but to stand on the pedals and we take it in turns to tuck into each other's slipstream in an attempt to gain some momentary respite.

Nearing the summit we pass the Simpson memorial – a set of steps leading away from the road to a concrete slab that marks where he fell in this barren, inhospitable land. The steps are part-hidden by the water bottles that have been laid in tribute to the man, a cyclist who lived fast and rode fast and always wanted to win the Tour, that most iconic of races. In turn, we climb the steps to take a photo and pay our respects. For Tour fans, especially those from the UK, this is a shrine, and it's a stark reminder of what this mountain demands, the sheer human effort required, for which Simpson paid the ultimate price. Then it's onwards for the final push, the road ramping up for the last stretch, steeper than seems possible. There's no breath left for words, and we fight our way up the remaining two hairpins where, after more than 20 kilometres of climbing and one last killer hook of a slope, the road finally levels off to reveal the summit, the observation tower, and the shop where our *Cinglés* cards will be stamped.

Ben, Nobby, Allen and Mark are there, jerseys ruffling in the wind.

'How you holding up, fella?' I ask Mark, whose vertigo is visibly distressing him. Being one of the first up the mountain can have its disadvantages; waiting around for everyone to regroup is not ideal for Mark's mental state. Though we're constantly ribbing Mark for being a selfish bastard, I can understand his need to take a selfie and get the hell out of there.

'Not good, mate. It's like being on Everest in a hurricane.'

Up here it's a different world. It seems unbelievable that the forest was so hot, and the valley so peaceful. It's a challenge even to stand up straight, and bikes must be held onto or blown to the ground. But the view is incredible, and wholly unique. We have grown accustomed to seeing the rain clinging to the surrounding peaks, to see a valley sunken within an endless landscape of Goliaths. Here there are no clouds, no mountain ranges. There is just Ventoux, and below, a carpet of toy villages, ribboning roads and endless green plains.

Yet we cannot linger. 'OK Peaky Climbers – back in the saddle!' This is only the beginning.

The road that crowns Ventoux is aptly named the Col des Tempêtes, *Storm Pass*, and we cross the apex and begin the descent to Malaucène into gusting winds of 50mph. The bicycles are tossed and spun like leaves across the road, weightless beneath us. Knuckles are white from gripping the bars, one foot unclipped in case we fall, each corner bringing yet another slap in the face. This is a nervous couple of kilometres. It's nigh on impossible to stay in control, and at one point Simon is blown entirely onto the wrong side of the road. There's an ear-splitting beep as a van careens past, swerving into the gravel to avoid a collision, with barely a chance to touch the brakes. Simon comes to a halt, his heart visibly pounding in his chest. The rider ahead has also stopped. 'I thought you were a goner,' he says. 'That was close.' Simon was about an inch away from not completing the week.

Once we reach a more sheltered part, JB and Ben are off, with Simon 'Hurricane' Haly in hot pursuit. I watch them disappear into the distance, envious of their easy speed. I don't have their belief to be able to pull it back, not trusting myself to fully let go of the brakes. Other cyclists are making the ascent, many of them walking. Round a corner, JB and Simon have stopped and are leaning over his bike, checking the brakes.

'Everything OK, fellas?'

'I could smell burning rubber and thought it might be the pads I fitted last night,' says Simon.

'But they're fine. It must be the cars.' There is a long stack of traffic inching its way down the mountain, the road too narrow for both riders and drivers.

'Held up by all the bloody cyclists,' says JB.

'Anyway, the wheel rims are nice and warm.' Simon wraps his cold fingers around the metal as I re-clip and resume the descent. A minute later they whizz past me again. 'Alright there, tortoise?' My manoeuvring is, let's say, careful. 'Just taking in the scenery!' I reply.

How Simon goes so fast downhill I will never understand. That incident with the van was not his first close call. Back in April we flew out to Mallorca for a full weekend of training, the first time we'd done back-to-back days of serious mountain climbing. On one of the descents JB had gone ahead, then Ben and Simon, then me, and as Simon gathered speed a goat jumped off the verge and just stood there, stock still, directly in his path. It was a split-second decision as to which way to go, left or right, and as he swerved one way the goat calmly stepped the other, at the exact moment that a car passed in the opposite direction. Everything just missed everything else. It was over in a matter of seconds, but it could easily have had a different outcome. Simon's descents have been a touch more cautious since Goatgate.

The café in Malaucène is buzzing with cyclists and tourists. *Cinglés* cards stamped, we queue up for coffee and yet another round of baguettes. Conversation is stunted as the thought of having to go back up again not once, but twice, hits us like a sledgehammer. Ben exhales through puffed cheeks; Nobby and Mark are chattering nervously. Allen excuses himself and goes to reapply the chamois cream to soothe the inevitable saddle sore.

'Anyone up for riding straight round to Sault from here?' JB asks. 'More coffee might be nice.' I suspect he's not entirely joking. 'We can just get the next stamp. No one would ever know.'

As the caffeine and food hits our systems the mood begins to lift, and a gentle buzz of motivation and encouragement builds among the eight of us. 'That was the best custard tart I have ever eaten,' says Simon. The smiles return, and soon we are ready for the next attempt.

The underlying apprehension remains, but with each ascent we are taking a chunk out of Ventoux. We know exactly what we will find at the summit, which makes it both easier and more difficult; though we know the climb is possible, we're also fully aware of how much of an effort it is. The forest hugs us once more, the slope slightly more forgiving on this stretch. Out of the trees we emerge onto the lunar landscape, this time a sprinkling of pine trees dancing on the blinding white rocks. Way above our heads the observation tower is clearly visible, drawing steadily closer as the road continues its energy-sapping slope. The wind blasts in our faces, and JB's grin has been replaced by a grimace. The sustained effort of up, up, up, and the three days of climbing preceding has finally taken its toll on his back. With each pedal stroke, he is flinching.

'You're doing great. Keep going,' I tell him. 'Nearly there.'

Just below the summit, JB and I are joined by Nobby, Simon and Ben, and we crawl collectively around the last few hairpins, this final stretch a massive battle of strength and wits against the gusts. The heavy wooden barriers that mark the lanes at the summit have blown over and the road is on the verge of being closed. JB eases himself off his bike and sinks onto the kerb, head bowed. This is concerning; he is usually so buoyant.

'My back is bloody killing me. I don't think I can do that again.'

'I have some Ibuprofen if you want it,' says Simon.

He takes the whole packet.

'You can do it. Come on buddy. One more time.'

Teamwork is what gets us to the peak each time, cajoling, supporting, encouraging each other. Our tactics for riding – whether that be all together, in small groups, or each man for himself – had been the most contentious issue since day one, and it wasn't until the challenge was just a couple of months away that things fell into place.

We had booked a long weekend in the Alps, the final test in our long list of milestones; after putting the work in, would our training stand up? The weather was stunning but scorching, with heavy, airless skies – great for sunbathing, but less good for cycling up mountains. We learned the hard way to conserve water, carefully rationing our ever-depleting supplies depending on how far it was to civilisation. Mark, who'd only brought one water bottle, ended up drinking from a mid-mountain stream. In the villages stood large stone troughs in which locals would traditionally wash vegetables and clothes as well as lead their cattle to drink; these became our saviours, where we would fill bottles and cool heads, and were dubbed 'Haly troughs' after Simon tried to climb in one.

One of the peaks on the schedule that weekend was the Col de la Madeleine, at over 2000m high and with an almost consistently double-figure gradient, renowned as being one of the most difficult in the Alps. There was no plan as such; we had vague notions of riding together, but with such a range of speeds, strengths and abilities, we would inevitably separate. Mark, as usual, was heading the pack, and as a group of svelte cyclists spun past, ('I wouldn't be that thin six months after I died,' said Simon) he was off in hot pursuit. Gradually the rest of the team spread out, separated by the slope, and Simon was left lagging behind. The dizzying heat grew more intense the higher we climbed, and though it was tough on all of us, it was doubly difficult for Simon, who had always suffered the most with the heat. The air was suffocating, the temperature unbearable and, unable to breathe with any efficiency, Simon was reduced to a miserable crawl, struggling with every pedal turn, his team mates long gone. Almost every cyclist in France seemed to overtake him, including an old woman tootling home with her *boulangerie* shopping.

Stopping partway up, I turned to take some video footage of JB and Ben riding past, then kept the camera rolling, expecting Simon to come around the corner at any moment. After a couple of minutes when he still hadn't emerged, I stopped filming. Something was clearly up. Maybe a mechanical, I hoped. Finally he appeared, and I flipped the camera back on.

'The gorilla appears in the mist,' I commentated as he inched his way towards me, his pedals turning so slowly as to be almost not moving. But the joke fell flat. It was clear that Simon was in serious trouble.

'Are you OK?' I asked as he eventually pulled level.

'Really – finding – this – difficult,' he managed, his face flushed with the effort and his jersey drenched in sweat. I passed him some water which he gulped between unsteady breaths.

'How much further?' he asked.

'Nearly at the lunch stop,' I said. We pulled away together, but Simon was soon far behind. I paused every so often to check he was OK, the remaining kilometres to the café never-ending. While ordering our food, we realised Mark was nowhere to be seen. 'I think he has gone on to the summit with his new friends,' Ben said.

'Really? Bloody hell.' I took out my phone and called him.

'Mark, do you realise what's going on back here? Simon is on the verge of collapse. It's not fair of you to race off like you did. Remember, we are a team. This is not about you.'

After reaching the summit, it was a short descent to the turning for the Col du Chaussy, and Simon was once again bringing up the rear. It had already taken every ounce of his energy and determination to reach the previous peak, and trundling up that mountain in the ever-rising heat was the point at which he decided he might not be cut out for the challenge after all. It wasn't just the climb, it was the burden of feeling that everyone was constantly waiting for him. Struggling up that slope by himself, all he could think about was quitting the team.

Partway up the climb we re-grouped.

'I'm having a really bad time.'

'Maybe you should drop back down the Madeleine? We can meet you at the hotel later.'

He took a few deep breaths.

'I'll keep going.'

As we remounted and gradually slid away up the hill, Mark stayed at Simon's side, quietly matching his pace, talking him through the climb. Hairpin after hairpin they tackled the relentless slope together, resolute and steady. When it finally arrived, they toasted the summit with a beer. It had been a true demonstration of teamwork, and as much a turning point for Mark as for Simon.

It was then that we decided to always ride in pairs. Never again would a Peaky Climber be left to deal with a climb on their own. Alone, thoughts of defeat can become deafening. Together, the struggle is halved.

These were the moments when the team was cemented, the moments of tribulation which forged the steel of our relationships. Those training runs had held such significance, not simply as a test of our physical and mental capabilities, but an exploration of teamwork and resilience. Emotions were laid bare, with everyone's quirks and weaknesses spread out for all to see. In the end, that's what made the Peakies. No man for himself.

The third ascent begins in Sault, back up the slope we just cruised down, and though the village is closest to the summit in terms of altitude, there are still 1200 metres to climb. We roll through acres of lavender fields, the smell lingering despite their having long since been harvested. Bundles of the flowers sit piled up outside roadside cafés, waiting to be sold.

'Beautiful,' says Simon, breathing in a perfume-laden lungful. 'Lavender is my favourite herb. It's a type of mint, did you know that?'

'More importantly, Simon, how did *you* know that?'

'Oh, well, I do my mother-in-law's garden.'

'Is that a euphemism?' Ben cackles.

'I keep the pub garden as well, at the Green Dragon.'

'You kept that quiet, Si.'

'Look out lads, we have Alan Titchmarsh among us!'

It seems fitting that the final attempt on Ventoux should be made as a group effort, and the greenery of the lower slopes encloses the eight of us in its warmth as we hit the climb together. Fire roads wander off between the trees and sheep graze the slopes. Le Chalet Reynard is once more reached, the only building on the mountain between the foot and the peak, used variously as a refuge and a restaurant, and the focal point for riders; it is often said, once you've reached Chalet Reynard you've cracked the climb. It's a struggle to see how that can be true. At 1400m high, the steepest part of the climb is over, yet the difficulties are just beginning. We pause, collecting ourselves before launching the last offensive.

The past four days have finally got to Allen. On any other day he is the model of politeness, but now, in pain, hungry and exhausted, lathered in four tubs of chamois fudge, he lets rip: 'I never want to see this fucking mountain again. Macca, you wanker, you can fuck right off if you ask me to do anything like this again.'

Astounded, there is silence, then we burst into gigantic rolling laughs.

'Allen, that was priceless!'

'You have become a true Peaky at last.'

Allen begins to laugh too, and with a Peaky Climbers badge to add to those in his Scout collection, he leads the way back into the climb, joining the familiar route of the Bédoin ascent. The laughter continues as we jump on our bikes and follow up the slope, at least for the first five metres, then it's back to cycling hard.

The last vestiges of the pine forest cling to the surface as the view opens up, and up we climb towards the observation tower, the whole of Provence laid out below. Graham takes the brunt of the wind, with Allen and Simon tucked in behind me. With one last nod to Tommy Simpson we reach the final few hairpins.

I turn to Simon.

'You take the glory, mate. Anniversary present.'

'You sure, Skip?'

'Absolutely. All part of the love we have for you, Si!'

Out he rides, straight into the roaring wind, Graham on his tail and they race the final corner, a sprint finish for the podium, Simon taking it by a head. All that training has paid off.

Allen turns the last bend as though he's cycling in treacle and as we cross the summit line for the third time he stops and breaks down, tears gushing down his cheeks. It's not just the physical pain, but a release of everything that's been building up throughout the past few months: the training, the commitment to the team and the underlying worry that these peaks would beat us. But here we are, at the top. I give him a quick hug and a pat on the back, then leave him to his reflections. This has been an immense day.

It's a jubilant group that gathers at the summit: we have completed the Day of Days. Dosed up on the pharmacy, JB is back to his usual bouncy self. Allen has now collected himself and Graham is actually smiling, which I think we captured on film. Ben keeps saying, 'I can't believe we just did that,' over and over. Mark is slapping backs and hugging everyone, Simon has his usual beaming smile and I stand there looking at the guys as proud as punch.

'That was nuts.'

We are all completely knackered, here for the final time, *Cinglés* achieved.

The glow of the climb quickly cools in the high wind, and Nobby has already begun to shiver. A Dutch rider we had seen before arrives at the summit. He is a *Cinglés* veteran, completing the challenge every year. He is dressed in just a t-shirt.

'He's mad!'

'I am wearing everything I own,' Ben says. 'I have the van upholstery on!'

Looking across the awesome landscape one last time, we line up for our summit photograph. This is what the training had been for, to conquer mountains such as this. To ride it once is hard, to ride it three times is even harder, to do it in the midst of a multi-day, multi-mountain challenge – that's just incredible for a bunch of novice riders. We lift our bicycles above our heads as the sun sets on Provence.

To our supporters, our fans, the people who were following the adventure on Facebook, the readers of the blog, it was all about those seven days in France. Whenever we told anyone what we were doing, it was always building up to this. This was what was splashed all over the publicity; this was what the press focussed on. But far from being the whole story, the ride itself was only the final part. For 12 months the challenge absolutely swamped our lives. With all the training, the spin classes, the gym sessions, the sportives, the milestones, the fundraising, the team meetings, the nutrition, the evenings at home with the turbo trainer, the long weekend rides, every damn waking hour was spent preparing for the ride. It became an obsession; we could never do enough, and always at the back of our minds was the question, 'Are we mad to attempt this?' Work took a back seat, even relationships. There were no holidays, no extras, no weekends away. I didn't walk the dog for a year.

When this all started I remember Nicola saying, 'So you're climbing a few mountains – big deal.' Neither she nor I had any idea of what it would truly involve, or the preparation that would go into it. Our whole lives together stopped. Any suggestion of doing anything was answered with, 'No, I have to train.' Shall we go rambling at the weekend? No, I have to train. Can we go out tonight? No, I have to train. If it wasn't to do with the Peaky Climbers, we couldn't do it. No drinking at Christmas, none at New Year, not at Nicola's birthday either. Any spare money was used to upgrade the bikes, and more than once it caused tension with partners.

Training took its toll: it was one hell of a beating for our bodies, and we were constantly hurting, riddled with niggling aches and pains, but more than that was the exhaustion that came with it. If I wasn't cycling or eating I was asleep.

About six months in, around the time that Ben was struggling and JB fell ill, and we were all beginning to appreciate the scale of the task we'd taken on, our partners came to a similar realisation. Like us, they had bonded as the project progressed, getting to know each other at our charity events, sometimes coming to meetings, and pinging messages around on WhatsApp.

'This is insane, and there are still months and months to go.'

'Simon has got new tyres, now Nobby wants them too. I can't believe how much they've spent on bloody tyres!'

'Doesn't he think *I* might want to go to Mallorca on a jolly with my mates?'

'He is always exhausted. I can't give him enough food, and every time he sits down he falls asleep.'

The sacrifices our partners made to get us to the start line was immense, and at no point during those early days had we realised just how much of an impact it would have on them. Life doesn't just stop because of a thing like this. While we were out there putting in the miles, Nicola, Nicky, Mandy, the Janes, Kirstie and Catherine were the ones holding everything else together. Staying at home was definitely not the easy option.

Day Five

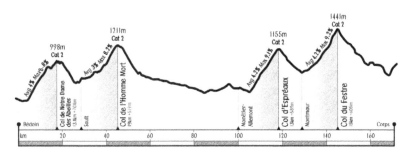

It is a day to celebrate more than others, for me at least: the day I turn 50. There will be no champagne for breakfast, no pool-side lounging and wine with the family, but yet more mountains to climb. Nicola had snuck some birthday cards into my luggage, and at breakfast there is the expected 'old man' banter, cards, balloons and a surprise chocolate tart baked by the host. After a particularly dodgy rendition of Happy Birthday, we head off to collect our bikes, where Simon attaches some balloons beneath my saddle. 'Alright, fellas. Let's go and climb some mountains.'

It's on days like this, those meaningful dates, that I think most of my mother. It's strange, ten years on, to have lived so much of my life without her, but for it to feel like no time at all. There is so much I have done since then, and I mourn the fact that she didn't have the chance to be a part of any of it. But it is her love, passion and belief in me that inspired these things to happen. Those parts of her live on through me and through the challenge we've undertaken. For that I owe her everything and I know she would have been so proud.

The Alpine passes are busy after the solitude of the Pyrenees. Accustomed to seeing cyclists on the roads, most drivers pass carefully, though some spare us precious little room, with a few risky overtakes on blind corners. It's usually Ben who engages them in conversation, a quick *bonjour* through an open window. Most don't believe that we're on our fifth consecutive day of climbing.

These roads would originally have been used to herd livestock over the mountains before being upgraded for military purposes. It seems mad that a cyclist would attempt what are essentially old goat tracks, created for creatures for whom the mountains are in their blood. Even when the armies came along, their soldiers would march like machines, traversing land far beyond the potential of mere mortals. Yet that is what Desgrange wanted when he first conceived of the Tour de France, to make heroes of his competitors in an event so difficult that those who finished would be elevated to the status of supermen. Those first riders struggled, burdened with heavy steel frames and a single fixed gear. Now, the professional peloton makes short work of such climbs, probably hitting summits in half the time of the original racers, aided by carbon fibre frames, training plans and perhaps other things we shouldn't mention. All things considered, this is utterly mad, completely bonkers, off the scale. Yet we are not the only cyclists here.

The human body is a wonderful thing in its adaptability; as the months passed, our average speeds gradually increased, as did our ease of climbing. By March we were on our way to Wales for a third time to take on the Tumble once more, though this time there would be two big climbs and almost 100 miles of riding as a warm-up. Despite legs and minds being heavy from a full day in the saddle, everyone made it to the top. Well, almost everyone. Stuart had turned back after the first hill and was waiting for us in the pub. The intention was still to take part in the challenge, but with everything going on at home, he barely had time to train, which compromised both his fitness and his family. Several times over the preceding months I'd taken him to one side: 'Listen, mate, the mountains will always be there. I know this is important to you and you don't want to let the team down, but please be realistic. You will only have this baby once. If Nicola told me she was pregnant, there's no way I would still be here.' But Stuart was not a quitter. Though this was one more milestone he was not going to make, he remained part of the team.

Our May training trip doubled as a visit to the Caring Cancer Trust holiday camp, which that year would take place on the Isle of Wight. Not only would we be hitting some hills and squeezing in the miles, we would meet the children who would directly benefit from our fundraising. Maisie Norton was forefront in our minds as we headed out for the 100 mile ride to Lymington and the ferry port.

Twenty miles in, Stuart turned to me. 'Macca, I'm not coming.'

'What do you mean?'

'I'm going to head back from here. You know, with the baby and everything.'

'It's a bit out of the blue, mate! We're already on our way.'

'Yes, I know. Sorry. I should have said something before.'

'Well, OK. You do what you gotta do.'

It had become almost predictable – I had given up being annoyed at Stuart. He looped back to spend time with his four week old son and a very disgruntled wife.

As the ferry pulled away from the mainland, the guys assembled around the table. It was a nervous gathering, the tension palpable. On the agenda, only one item.

'OK. We all know there's a problem here that needs sorting. What does everyone feel we should do about Stuart?'

'He hasn't been hitting the milestones. He's doing about half the distance everyone else is doing.'

'But with a new baby and a one-year-old at home it's bound to be tough on him.'

'His new job is pretty high-pressure as well.'

'What if he still takes part, and just doesn't ride all the peaks?'

'You can't be half-hearted about this.'

'Being half-in wouldn't be fair on anyone, Stuey or the rest of us.'

'You're in, completely committed, or you're out. And I think he should be out. I love Stuey to bits but to be honest, he should have quit ages ago.'

'I agree. I know we don't like it but I think the answer's obvious.'

To discuss removing a founding member from the team was distinctly uncomfortable. But Stuart wasn't the type to fall on his sword – we would have to make the decision for him. It was unanimous. A difficult meeting was to follow.

Later that day the Peaky Climbers gathered on the beach for a game of football with the kids from the Caring Cancer Trust. 'Come on, mate, run!' yelled Mark as he passed the ball to a young lad of around 15, a tall boy with legs seemingly too long for his body and a huge smile. We'd had a frank meeting with Ian and Chris, the directors of the charity, who had told us not to feel sorry for the children or to wrap them up in cotton wool. Instead, we should treat them as we would any other person. Mark might have taken this too far. 'I've only got one lung!' the boy replied.

As evening settled over the beach and the fading pink of the sun caught the wind-rippled sea, we retreated to the fire pit, where crackling sticks sent sparks winding into the twilight sky. Our sponsors Clive and Steve, and Nicola and Jai as well as JB's wife Mandy had journeyed out to join us, and together with the children and staff from the Trust, the conversation burbled into the night. In the glow of the fire, Nobby struck up on the guitar, joined by Jai, and as night fell, a singalong began.

'I can't believe how stoical these kids are,' murmured Mark. 'I'm in awe.'

'They're pretty mature for such young kids,' said JB. 'It's really inspiring.'

As the weekend progressed, and we joined the group in their games and heard their stories, our admiration grew. Interspersed was some terrific cycling, with plenty of hills and some beautiful coastal miles. JB finally found his rhythm, consciously standing up out of the saddle on the climbs, which did wonders for his back. 'You look like a different rider,' Nobby said. For Allen, who really felt at home with the young people – unsurprising, given his experience as a Scout Leader – it brought out a more confident side that we had not seen before.

Most of all, meeting those children, hearing their stories and seeing their positivity, transformed our mission. No 'woe is me' tales, they were down to earth and full of happiness. Many remembered Maisie. Encountering real people who would directly benefit from our fundraising meant a lot to us and brought the whole challenge to life, and it would also give us an extra kick up all those mountains when the time came.

Graham happened to be there that weekend riding with us. A mate of Ben's from rugby (watching, not doing), he had tagged along to boost his training for a coming three-day race to Paris. And so it happened that his involvement coincided with Stuart's departure. We were all reeling from losing Stu – it didn't seem right to be approaching the challenge with a lopsided team, and there was much talk in the days following the Isle of Wight trip about whether to continue as a seven-piece or invite another player. Did we actually need eight? Would anyone brought in at this stage fit in with the banter and the team dynamic? But everything so far had centred on our being an octet, and we came to a team decision. We would invite Graham to be our eighth man.

He was fairly pliable when I called him, on a golfing holiday in Scotland, red wine in hand, which possibly helped in his agreement, though Anna, his wife, took more convincing: this would be yet another event in an already packed calendar of sporting activities. But how could he say no to such an invitation? Already a more-than-capable cyclist with many long-distance, multi-day rides to his name, he would have no trouble in terms of the physical preparation. Not only would the cycling be terrific, he would be able to contribute to the team from a position of experience. Fitting into our existing programme and raising the necessary funds might be a challenge, but after a couple of days' consideration, Graham accepted our offer.

The first outing with our new line-up was to London, where we were to take part in the RideLondon sportive, a 100-mile ride from Stratford in east London, through the Surrey hills, to the doorstep of Buckingham Palace. We stayed with JB's sister in Islington where, after only a handful of hours' sleep, we arose for a breakfast cooked by Ollie, JB's nephew, who had just arrived home after a night out. And that's when Graham took the brunt of some banter, earning himself the nickname 'Morrisey' on account of his extreme morning misery. His induction to the Peaky Climbers was complete.

It had been Simon's idea that we should all take part; this was his kind of ride, flat and fast, and we took it in turns to push the Peaky peloton, surging through the London suburbs to the country lanes that would rise and fall along the edge of the North Downs. Mostly it was Simon, Mark and Graham who led the charge, though JB, Ben, Allen and I did our bit under duress. Over the course of the 100 miles we got to know Graham: married but no children, adoring of his dog, a lover of red wine – a quaffer rather than a connoisseur – and a fair bit happier than first thought. The three famous climbs, Uplands Corner, Leith Hill and Box Hill, passed as mere blips to our progress, and we powered up each in our newly-printed team jerseys splashed with our charities and sponsors. The support of the crowd carried us forwards, and we looked and felt every bit the professionals. In nine short months we had progressed from the ramshackle chancers who battled to complete *Ay Up! Yorkshire* to the confident and celebratory group that lined up side by side on The Mall to sail across that finish line.

The sun sits warm on our backs as we head towards our first climb of the day, over the Col de Notre Dame des Abeilles.

'Nice of the sun to show up.'

'Is that what that yellow thing is in the sky?'

'Looks like the weather gods put in a word for your birthday, Macca.'

'This is more like it,' says Nobby, looking relaxed for a change, stretching out like a cat soaking up the rays. It's a relief not to have to brace ourselves against the elements, but instead sit tall on our saddles and allow the light breeze to propel us through the miles. The route weaves alternately through wide open farmland where mountain peaks rise sharply from the plains, and up through settlements that sit piled on top of themselves on the mountainside. Lakes emerge, hidden in the valley folds, their surfaces reflecting the cornflower sky. With only the odd whiff of cloud, it is a glorious day.

'Would you take a look at that view,' says Graham as we make our way through a magnificent gorge, the road twisting between overhanging cliff faces as the river winds below. 'Riding your bike doesn't get much better than this.'

The villages come and go, and seeing the locals go about their daily business makes a pleasant change from riding through the deserted ski resorts and ghost towns of the bigger, more iconic climbs. In each village we stop at the Haly Troughs and fill our bottles; after so much shocking weather it takes time to attune to the heat. Mont Ventoux does not let us go easily, looming large on the periphery for much of the day, and remaining in our legs long after having disappeared from view. Ben, though, is still buzzing: 'Coming down that last time was insane,' he says. 'I would happily have climbed Ventoux a fourth time just for that descent.'

The thermometer creeps ever upwards as we climb. This is bad news for Simon, whose sprint finish for the Cinglés podium is also taking its toll. Nobby holds back to keep him company.

With short climbs and low average gradients the ride looked easy on paper, but with four days and nine cols under our wheels it is anything but smooth. Physical niggles are building, and saddle sore, that delightful side-effect of perching on a tiny strip of leather all day, means that some of the team have already stopped for their second application of chamois cream. Each day we say, 'That was the hardest,' and this is no exception. It feels hotter for being the only hot day, it feels longer for coming after Ventoux, and it is the furthest any of us have ever cycled.

In hindsight, I should have scheduled a rest day, or at least a morning off. Even the pros have a breather after their mountain stages, but not us – my fault, bad planning. It would have been great to have some time to recover from what we'd put our bodies through, and to reflect on what had been the best days of cycling any of us had ever experienced.

But no, for the Peaky Climbers it's onwards and upwards.

The first climb dealt with, we settle into the ascent of l'Homme Mort, and as we struggle up the short, steep section to the summit, a sharp pain appears in my left knee. It had been niggling earlier in the day, but until this moment I could ignore it. There is definitely no ignoring it now. I hop off the bike and rub in some pain relief gel, which does the trick. But at the back of my mind I'm worried – this is what I had feared might happen.

The knee trouble began about four weeks before the challenge: nothing major, but a noticeable amount of discomfort, enough for me to go for a bike fitting – my third in the past year – just to be safe. All was in good order, and I tapered my training to give my knees plenty of time to rest and recover after the amount of bashing I had put them through. It was such a relief to remain trouble-free for the first four days, and to experience no discomfort other than the usual aches and pains.

But now, things don't feel right. It has only been a few hours but my fifties are already a whole lot harder than my forties.

After the descent of l'Homme Mort there is a 40 kilometre ride to our lunch stop along the valley floor and the Peaky peloton pushes on, with Mark, Graham, Nobby, Allen and Ben relishing the beautiful ride and some easy speed. But poor Simon is having a really hard time. This would have been his dream ride, an easy zoom along the gently undulating valley floor, but it is torment in the stifling heat. JB and I try to pace him back to the rest of team, and in order to make a dent in the distance I do what I never do, and ride in a high gear. Even on the team speed training rides, when we took it in turns to lead out the peloton, I was always Captain Slow, never able to maintain the speed that the others had set, never quite recovering my breath before the next stint at the front. But here, the need to reach the others clouds my judgement. After 20 kilometres or so of pushing hard, I feel my knee go. Stupidly I continue riding in the same way, heaving against the gear, ignoring the sensible voice telling me to reduce the pressure and ride at a quicker cadence. By the time we arrive at the café for lunch my left knee is in a considerable amount of pain. It's a case of more pain relief gel and more paracetamol, but with two climbs remaining, and two full days after that, I am seriously worried about how I'll be able to continue, the worst possible birthday present being an enforced day off.

Lunch is a nightmare. We're on a tight schedule, with another 80 kilometres to ride before reaching our evening B&B, but our café is a glorified burger van in a marquee and isn't coping well with the crowds. It's tempting to push on without eating, but we've made that mistake before, back on our Alpine training trip, when, in the interests of time, we skipped lunch before scaling the Glandon. We thought it would be OK – feeling strong, with pockets full of snacks, we hit the slope. But in such extreme heat we were soon struggling. In typical fashion, Mark had no food with him, so I gave him mine, and three kilometres from the summit, I bonked. 'Dizzy' was Peaky talk for bonking, that athletes' nightmare of running into fuel deficiency, with Mark the most frequent recipient of a rousing chorus of 'Dizzy… my head is spinning…' from the rest of us. Now it was my turn. And bonking is not nearly as fun as it sounds. Against an average 10% gradient I battled the last kilometres, feeling as though I were cycling in quicksand, arms and legs shaking, the blood scraping at the walls of my veins for any iota of sugar, concentration blown, mouth dry, vision blurring. Finally, miraculously, the summit appeared, and through the blur emerged the mirage of a tuck shop, which became more and more real as we ground our way towards it. Crisps! Chocolate! Coke! We stuffed our faces while embracing Fabrice, the shop owner, as the Peakies' new BFF. When we finally stopped for a proper lunch on the descent of the Col de la Croix de Fer, Mark got a ticking off. He had learned his lesson and completed the challenge with more food than an ASDA warehouse.

Nobby has been struggling to eat enough all week. Vegetarianism just isn't a thing in France. Dinner is spaghetti with olive oil if you're lucky, and he spends half his time in the restaurants trying to convince the waiter that no, he can't eat ham. Amazingly, there's a veggie burger on the menu today but by the time it arrives, undercooked and 15 minutes late, he's given up and just has chips – not ideal given the distance we have left to go.

The rest of the team seem to be on good form as we begin the afternoon's ride, so I keep my knee troubles to myself, quietly sitting on Graham's wheel as we head towards the third climb of the day, Col d'Espréaux. This is the first climb of the entire trip that I haven't enjoyed. The heat is ridiculous and it's a massive struggle to stay with the group when I'm in so much pain. With a misplaced sense of pride I grin and bear it, not letting on to the others, regularly stopping for more gel. It's so frustrating. I'm fitter than I have ever been and I would have stormed these climbs if it weren't for the damn knee.

By the time we reach the Col du Festre I am reduced to a slow crawl. Still I keep quiet about the underlying issue, trying to smile as best I can. The team never leaves my side. The final few kilometres are excruciating and the relief of the descent can't come quickly enough. As we freewheel towards the hotel, the sun slowly sinks towards the horizon in a blistering explosion of colour, one of the most dramatic sunsets we have ever seen, and my mind finally wanders, away from the pain, to appreciate the magic of it all. With the whole valley painted in gold and the distant peaks glowing pink, our shadows grow longer as we descend. The intense heat has retreated to leave a warm breeze. This is what it was all for, moments such as this, feeling the freedom, drama and awe of the mountains, and to experience it as brothers in arms. The pain is temporarily forgotten as the descent spirals us from the mountainside towards our accommodation where, after four peaks, 170km and almost 12 hours in the saddle, we can all sit down and finally raise a glass for my birthday.

We are reaching our limit. We were expecting to have to dig deep, but this is unthinkably hard. It's a relentless slog of early starts, late finishes, never being able to eat enough food, passing out with exhaustion at the end of the day and being roused from sleep after what seems like no time at all. Once one peak is done it's straight on to the next, regardless of the weather or how little we have been able to recover. Each day we fall behind schedule, and it is often dark as we roll into our B&B. It's more physically punishing than we ever considered, and there is barely any time to contemplate the madness of it all. There is no rest, no respite. This part of things we did not train for.

Day Six

Corps – Saint-Jean-de-Maurienne

Distance 1154km Elevation gain 3550m

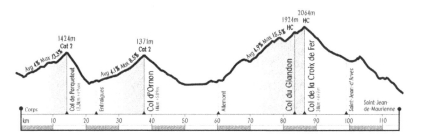

There's a wonderful sense of peace as we tackle the first climb of the morning, steadily ascending on tree-lined lanes through the French countryside, the road shared only by the occasional tractor and contemplative cow. Away from the main drag, we have space to think. The air is still and the overcast sky cool. Despite the soreness and the tiredness, all are in good spirits. It is a new day. As we progress higher up the Col de Parquetout the valley drops away in folds of green, with pine and beech cloaking the slopes. Ramshackle collections of houses and farm buildings cluster the road at times, and with views of the valley and the peaks beyond, this is vying for the most beautiful climb of the week. The scale of the surroundings is immense, and we crawl upwards like ants in a playground of giants. Dosed up to the eyeballs, my knee is holding up. Ben finds the legs to hit the summit ahead of the rest of us – his first time to do so – and he high fives us as we gradually join him.

Ben had taken to running to boost his training, narrowly being beaten to the Goring 10k finish line by two guys dressed as a camel. But heading out to Mallorca, with only four months to go, the weight still hadn't come off.

'This is nuts,' he confessed to Simon while climbing the Puig Major. 'Nothing seems to be working. I can't believe with all this training I'm not losing weight. It feels as though I'm carrying a small child up each hill!'

Simon laughed. 'I know what you mean! That's not going to make it any easier. How about the Marine Commando diet? It's basically eggs, eggs and more eggs for a couple of weeks. I'm sure the Marines don't actually endorse it, but I've heard it works.'

'That sounds bloody horrendous. OK, I'll try. Catherine is going to hate it!'

'Let's have a weigh-in in a fortnight.'

'You're on.'

So Ben was on eggs, lean meat, fruit and salad for two weeks, drinking only black coffee, water and lemon juice. 'How's it going?' we asked him after a few days. 'Catherine is slightly worried,' he said. 'She says no one should eat that many eggs! It's not great for nutrition but it seems to be working.'

And it really did. 'Ben looks trim,' said Nicola after one meeting at the Fox. As the weight fell off, the ease of climbing increased, his heart rate lowered and his stamina improved. There was no longer any doubt about Ben's ability to complete the challenge. It was as though he was a different person. His self-confidence was through the roof, and his beaming smile accompanied each training ride. By the time we reached the start line, Ben had lost three stone.

'Mind if I go, Skipper?' Mark asks as we crowd the Parquetout summit signpost, keen as usual to get back to the safety of ground level as soon as the photograph is taken.

'No problem,' I say. 'Are the climbs getting any easier?'

'It's fine unless there's a sheer drop. Going down is the difficult part,' he replies as he sets off. This descent is renowned for being the most technical of the Tour de France – steep, bumpy and very narrow. It's not long before I overtake Mark as he carefully manoeuvres down the hairpins, nice and slow, hugging the inside verge. Nobby is similarly cautious – though a terrific climber, he's not a fan of the descent. Ben, Simon and JB soon come whizzing past, quickly disappearing over the lip of the hill, crouched low on the saddle, fingers poised over the brakes, tyres bouncing over the rough tarmac. It's a skill that has improved even during the week, the ability to pick a perfect line and steer round each corner without hitting the deck.

The favourable weather, of course, doesn't last. Obviously blazing sunshine was too much to ask for the south of France and as we near the summit of the Col D'Ornon the first drops of rain begin their patter. By the time we've made the descent and sat down for lunch we are all completely soaked, and with no heating in the café, there's no chance to dry out. We grow colder as the meal goes on, shivering in our sodden layers as we wait for a break in the clouds so we can get moving again. The rain only lashes harder. As tourists enter the café to shelter from the elements, we give up and head back outside. The Croix de Fer has to be climbed, no matter what the conditions. This will be a long ascent, with a detour to the Glandon summit before we reach the famous Iron Cross.

It's confession time. It is obvious I am struggling, and I owe it to the lads to be straight with them.

'These last few climbs have been agony. My left knee has really taken the hit of all this climbing and I'm in a serious amount of pain.'

'Do you need some pain relief?'

'I've been using that gel as much as I can, which is helping a bit.'

'How about you stop and take a rest?'

'That's tempting! But I don't want to let you guys down. I'll keep going, but I won't be beating anyone to the summit the state I'm in.'

'Just take it steady, Skipper.'

Forcing cold hands back inside damp gloves, we prepare our bikes. Allen has changed into a very fetching pair of bright green and purple cycling shorts, his spares still damp from washing the previous day. The initial kilometres are miserable, the body fighting to generate heat, the wind blowing rain in horizontal sheets across the road. It's hard to truly prepare for these conditions. Though we took every piece of advice going, none of the guides tell you what it's like when you're wet through, wearing five layers, and still cold.

JB is lumped with me, Captain Slower-than-usual, with Ben, Graham, Simon and Allen in close proximity. The pain relief has long worn off and I'm grimacing with each pedal stroke, practically cycling one-legged. 'Ma, Pa,' JB prays, 'I know you're enjoying your retirement up there, but could you put in a word to Big G about the weather?' He cycles ahead to check on the others, turning his glove into a puppet which says, 'Hello' in a high-pitched voice as he passes. It does the trick – they're in hysterics. Soon he's back at my side. 'Doing OK, Mr Mac?' he asks. I grunt. The strategy of only pushing with one leg seems to be working, for now.

The winding road turns and climbs sharply to the Lac du Verney, the first of the two hydro-electric reservoirs that mark this climb. We ride alongside the great concrete dam that holds back the water, the reservoir beyond pocked with raindrops and swirling with wind. The EDF cables crackle under the falling water, and we leave the reservoir and loop up into the forest.

Not long after this, my right knee goes. It literally pops, and I stop suddenly with a sharp expletive. JB turns and waits. The slow trundle resumes. Guilt starts to niggle away; the guys are being a loyal support group, but at such a slow pace there's no chance for anyone to get warm. Graham is suffering the most, shivering uncontrollably, his breathing laboured. Riding in pairs was always intended to protect the individual, but that very ethic is now putting Graham in jeopardy. If he doesn't increase the revs right now he might not make it at all.

'You go ahead, Graham. Don't wait for me – I'll be fine.'

'I'm not happy about leaving you, mate.'

'It doesn't make sense having two of us in trouble.'

Graham's stubbornness is a testament to how much the team has changed him. I must confess, it took me a while to warm to Gray. A fiercely independent character, at first he would ride for himself, at his own speed, and I was initially firm with him about his commitment to the team. It must have been difficult to fit into a group that had formed such bonds throughout the year, especially with us all so slick with banter – he would often look on in bemusement as the rest of us tore each other to pieces. But as he settled in, he began to use his expertise to aid the team, not be independent of it. The kinds of struggles the rest of us were facing had never affected Graham, and witnessing, dealing with, and helping the team had a profound effect on him. He joined the Peaky Climbers as an individual, but he came out a true team player.

Ben also tells Graham to get going for the good of his health. We practically have to shout at him, and finally he agrees and heads on up the hill, rapidly disappearing into the mist. Allen and Simon have already cracked on, and Ben slides away too, trying to work some warmth into his limbs. JB holds back, wanting to talk me through the climb as I did for him on Ventoux. For his own benefit I tell him to bugger off.

It takes over an hour to reach the halfway point: the village of Rivier d'Allemont. Through sporadic gaps in the cloud, the rest of the team can be seen making their way up the climb, a long way ahead. Graham must have caught up with Nobby and Mark by now. Shortly after the village comes the dreaded patch of downhill, a short, sharp section of plunging altitude that makes the Croix de Fer so feared by cyclists and contributes to the deceptively low average gradient. Not only is it frustrating to lose the hard-won altitude, the downhill is long enough to cool muscles and further freeze the body. For Mark, who always works on a feet-left-to-climb rather than distance-left-to-travel basis, to lose all that elevation so quickly is a massive psychological blow.

The road kicks upwards again, instantly finding a double-figure gradient, and it's a struggle to keep the wheels turning. This is the most pain I have been in, ever. Standing on the pedals gives some brief respite, but all told, the climb is unbearable.

In a strange and sudden moment of calm, the rain stops. The prayers that JB was offering up must have worked, and a deep peace settles on the mountain, a suggestion of warmth returning to the air. Ahead I can see a cyclist, and it's Allen, dropping back to check that I am alright.

'Thanks mate. I'll survive.'

He heads off into the dissipating mist. Kestrels circle high above.

The second reservoir, the Lac du Grande Maison, appears ahead, an exquisite expanse of turquoise high up in the mountains, but my eyes are now closed to the view. The last resort is to talk myself through it. Expletives echo through the empty slopes, breaths ripping through lungs. I'm doing this for Mum, who couldn't physically inhale the air that's heaving through me. I'm doing this for Maisie, who kept her adventurous spirit to the last. Tears of pain stream down my cheeks, my balance swayed by bouts of dizziness as I push down on one agonising pedal after another.

The guys have long since reached the turning for the Col du Glandon, the first of the two summits to tick off on this climb. Graham ended up sprinting past Mark and Nobby, barely acknowledging them, so fixated was he on reaching the top. But the speed didn't help much and he was practically hyperventilating with cold when he got there, unable to do anything other than lean on his bike in distress. Nobby arrived shortly afterwards, having peeled away from Mark to give chase as Graham zoomed past. He found Graham in the van, shivering, thawing his frozen feet, weeping with the cold-addled guilt that his assigned role of domestique had been abandoned in the interests of survival. No one held this against him, of course, and Nobby climbed in to give him a hug.

The vans are parked outside the café where the Glandon and Croix de Fer cols meet. It's a steep 500m to the Glandon summit and I struggle up after having sobbed a few tears of my own, this time of pain.

And soon everyone is crying: to everyone's amazement, Simon's dad is waiting at the summit. 'Bob!' In our delirium, it's impossible not to well up as we take it in turns to hug him. 'What are you doing here?'

He laughs. 'I just had to see you out here. You guys have worked so hard for so long, I wanted to do something extra to help now you're actually on the road. It's been quite a challenge trying to figure out where you might be without letting on.'

'You mean you kept it a secret? Simon, did you know about this?'

'Not a thing!'

'Not even my wife knew!' says Bob.

The presence of someone from the 'real' world has a strange effect on us all. Our trip is no longer a series of sound bites and smiling photos posted on Facebook, a glammed-up version for our followers. Bob has seen the brutal reality, felt the frozen cloud biting at his cheeks, breathed in the scale of the mountains, witnessed our suffering. 'I had no idea it would be this tough,' he says in an aside to me as we gather for the summit photo. 'It was a good ten minutes after Graham got up here that he could speak. And he's the most experienced rider, so I began to wonder what state the rest of you would be in.'

This summit is familiar – we reached it on our Alpine

training trip, after climbing the Glandon ascent in its entirety – though no Haly Troughs are needed today. The training rides that got us to this point seem like a distant memory, those easy 80-milers full of sun, fun and laughter, coffee stops and good weather, with lovely views and a few hills thrown in to test ourselves. What a difference we have found. We have to physically hold Graham upright for the photo. 'How could the forecasters have got it so wrong?' Nobby manages through numb lips. 'Today I went to my dark place,' Ben says, 'but it was so cold and wet I didn't stay long.'

For Simon, though, it's as though a light has been switched on. Bob arrived at the right moment. Full of adrenaline at seeing his dad, he shoots off with Nobby and Mark as they push onwards for the remainder of the Croix de Fer. The sun is blinding but cold, and above a cloud-filled valley we climb the final few kilometres. I feel in my back pocket the edges of a letter from Maisie's dad, which was given to every team member to give an extra boost in these really tough moments. Many remained un-read, but having them there was enough, a reminder that this was about something greater than our current suffering. In excruciating pain, the two kilometres feel like 20, and this time, when JB stays at my side, I don't tell him to go away. I couldn't have done it without him.

The descent is freezing cold and miserable, with wind penetrating sodden jackets, and fingers quickly seizing up. The speedometer creeps upwards as we hurl ourselves down the mountainside. Everyone is desperate to reach the hotel. It looks as though we'll get there at a decent time tonight, giving us a welcome chance to dry out. Like many of the others I only have one pair of shoes and I'm keen to get them on the radiator. Graham has doubled his jacket with one of Ben's, and borrowed an extra pair of gloves, but still, the cold has settled into our bones and won't be shaken for hours. Six kilometres shy of the hotel, a sign appears by the side of the road: *route barrée*. No one speaks French but we can work it out. Regardless, we ignore it: road closures often don't affect cyclists. A short while later we roll up to a couple of concrete blocks, fencing, and padlocks. It appears impassable.

'Damn it. Which way now?'

'Maybe it's to stop people coming up?' suggests JB.

'Bet this wasn't on the spreadsheet,' Ben says.

JB ignores him. 'I'll see if we can get through.'

Bikes are hoiked above heads and passed over the fencing, which JB has managed to squeeze around. We gradually collect on the closed side and roll a little further down the road, soon stopped once more by piles of rubble and a couple of diggers sitting on the carriageway. The entire surface has been removed, damaged by the recent rains. Stacks of stone wait at the side to be laid in replacement. There's a walkway along the edge and JB and Ben shoulder their bikes to climb along it, ever optimistic that we might be able to continue. Ahead lies more rubble and more diggers, but no road.

'Fellas, this is dangerous. We are definitely not getting past.'

It's been a waste of time and has only made us colder. The hotel is frustratingly close. But we cannot pass.

Peter and Jack arrive in the vans. We explain the situation and they look up an alternate route: 25km over another two cols. There's no way we're riding that. Everyone piles into the vans.

It's nearing 8pm when we finally pull up to the hotel, sullen, miserable and frozen. Nobby has reached a new low. Our early finish and the luxury of a relaxed evening have slipped away and yet again it's pitch black by the time we arrive, and though we're desperate to get in and get dry, the vans need to be unloaded, so the warmth has to wait. My knees have totally seized up after 30 minutes sitting crammed in the van and I can barely walk to my room. JB helps by carrying my food box as I shuffle behind him.

'Where's Cricky?'

Mark has been conspicuously absent from proceedings.

'Shower, probably.'

'You're kidding! I'll kill him, selfish git...'

Nobby, Mark's long-suffering roommate, gets his own back by ceremoniously arranging his cycling kit over the whole of the only radiator in their room that works.

Day Seven

Saint-Jean-de-Maurienne – Alpe d'Huez

Distance 109km Elevation gain 4104m

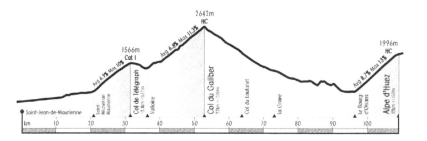

'JB, mate, do you mind, er, coming in here for a moment?'

I'm sitting on the throne, in perfect morning indignity, stuck fast. My knees are knackered to the extent that I can't lever myself upwards off the toilet.

We cackle at the ridiculousness of it all as he hauls me into an upright position, but beneath the laughter lies a significant worry. If I can't get off the toilet, how am I going to get up three mountains?

Yesterday evening I had grabbed a bucket of ice from the hotel bar to ease my swollen joints, but I had awoken in agony after a restless night, both knees burning with pain. I shuffle around the room gathering my kit, then limp down the stairs to breakfast, supporting myself on the bannister rail, feeling every bit the invalid. It's deeply depressing to have made it this far, through the spirit-bashing early starts, the terrible weather, the back-to-back mountain climbs, the sheer lunacy of it all, and to fall at the final hurdle. Just three peaks remain between us and the completion of this epic challenge. The final day is here.

But there's nothing I can do. I have pushed as hard as I can, and my body is screaming for me to stop. Though this is not what I would want, not what I had in mind on those long training runs through the Oxfordshire countryside, I have to put my long-term health first. More importantly, I have to put the others in the team first. Graham was in real trouble yesterday, and it's not OK to continue making everyone's lives difficult by being so slow and far behind. It's with a heavy heart I come to the decision not to ride.

I look ridiculous as I drag myself into breakfast.

'Morning, John Wayne!' The guys give me a roasting as I ease into a chair. Once the laughter subsides I break the news.

'It's obvious I'm going to struggle to cycle anywhere today. Things have been getting worse over the last two days and, as you know, I was in agony on the ride yesterday. You've all been amazingly supportive but it's not fair of me to keep slowing you down. There's no doubt all of you will hit the big ones today, but for me it's not going to happen. I have been agonising over this, but I have to be realistic. I'm not going to ride.'

Murmurs ripple around the table; no one wants this, but we

can't have a repeat of yesterday's fiasco.

'I'll ride in the van and give you some motivation.'

'I bet you'll love that! Yelling at us while you sit back and relax.'

'Skipper's prerogative!' I return. 'Speaking of which, shouldn't you lot be getting ready? Chop chop, no time to waste!'

There's a bustle of activity as everyone sets off to prepare for their day. JB claps a hand on my shoulder as he leaves the room, and Mark pauses for a moment.

'You've done us proud this week, mate' he says. 'It's been an incredible adventure and we couldn't have done it without you. You'll be missed today; it already feels like there's a hole in the team.'

'Thanks Cricky, that means a lot. But it's not just me who made this happen, it's all the hard work and dedication you lot have put in. You should all be so proud of yourselves; I couldn't have asked for a better crew.'

As the breakfast room empties, I remain seated, working through everything in my mind. If anything, I feel relief. I had been worried about telling the guys of my decision – more worried about that than I was about myself. Everyone is disappointed, but having their understanding and sympathy has made me a lot calmer. Though honestly, I'm gutted: the Col du Télégraphe and the Col du Galibier were the two climbs to which I'd been most looking forward, both iconic in the Tour de France, with the Galibier, rising to more than 2500m, by far the highest pass this week. It would have been spectacular to stand at the peak, having taken on a mountain viewed by many as the greatest climb in France.

But it's not to be. Today my role will be that of manager. It might be fun, actually, to do what I used to do in my football days, loud-mouthing from the sidelines. I hobble out to the vans and await the team, overwhelmed with emotion, not because I'm not riding, but because these seven men have become brothers over the course of the year, and to see them here, achieving what we all questioned was possible at various times, is hugely moving.

The road rises up the Col du Télégraphe, winding through the forest. It's perfect climbing weather: no rain, light breeze, patchy clouds. Light plays on the tarmac, and flashes of the valley and the surrounding peaks are caught between the trees as the van rumbles upwards. Every so often we overtake a cyclist, and when we spot one of ours, the yells begin: 'Atta boys! Come on you Peakies!' They look resplendent in their kit, grinding up that slope, faces plastered with smiles, and I am bursting with pride. They yell abuse as much as asking after my wellbeing. We pull over to set up a pit stop, handing out snacks and drinks as they pass.

With a beep, a car pulls up behind us. It's Stuart, who has driven most of the night to be there for the final day.

'Stuey! What a star!' I say, grabbing him in a big hug.

'What happened to you?' he asks. I explain the situation. 'Tough break, buddy,' he says.

'Came along for a ride, did you?' I ask, giving him a playful dig in the ribs.

'That's right. Bike's in the boot. Thought I'd take the glory of your last few climbs,' he replies. 'Seriously though, it's a pleasure to see the team on the slopes. They've done a terrific job.' Stuart looks down the road, lost in self-reflection, and it's clearly tough for him to be here. To have been involved from the beginning, to have invested so much time and emotion, to have been part of the team and known that bond that we all felt, but to not be doing the actual challenge, must be overwhelmingly hard. We all shared his pain, went through his heartache. I pat him on the back. 'You'll always be a Peaky, mate,' I say.

It takes a while for us to catch Nobby and Graham, who are hitting the climb hard. Throughout the seven days these two have been massive team players, both sacrificing their own ambitions for the benefit of the team, holding back and supporting the others up the climbs. It was about time to let them off the leash. 'Green light on this climb, fellas; go for it,' I had told them at the bottom.

Nobby is climbing with ease as we approach. 'Looking strong, Nobby!'

'Feels terrific,' he says, grinning.

A short while later we overtake Graham, snaking his way upwards with confidence. 'Go on Graham! Give it the beans!' He raises his hand as we pass and gives the thumbs up. The pair of them are on sparkling form and it's a pleasure to see them riding so well.

We pull up at the summit to await the team. The mountain is thick with pines, and a rich green spreads back down the valley while snow-topped peaks rise ahead. We're not waiting long before Nobby and Graham arrive, racing each other in a sprint finish around the corner. 'Well done, you two!'

'That was fantastic,' says Graham, 'I really enjoyed it. But you know, even though I've been wanting to push hard all week, I think my favourite climbs have been the ones ridden at a steady pace whilst chatting and joking. That's not something I've really done before. It definitely gives you a different perspective.'

'Yeah, same,' says Nobby. 'We missed the team!'

Gradually the others arrive and we take our summit photograph. It's then a five kilometre descent before the climb up the giant begins.

The *muletier* goat track that once traversed the Galibier, then the rough-paved military road that replaced it, would have gone straight over the top, the gradients nothing for those Roman armies that would have marched it. Over time it has been modified and lengthened to make the climb less severe, but still, when the Tour de France pioneers crossed it in 1911 it was higher, harder and colder than anything any of them had ever experienced. And it's the same for the Peaky Climbers. It was as Tour de France founder Desgrange said: 'Are these men not winged, who today climbed to heights where even eagles don't go… they rose so high they seemed to dominate the world!'

Once more, I watch the team wind their way up the mountain, catching flashes of their yellow-sleeved jerseys in the distance. As the road climbs ever higher, twisting back and forth up the switchbacks, the trees thin out, soon disappearing altogether, leaving nothing to shelter the slopes from the bracing wind. It's a harsh and barren landscape, full of browns and greys and burnt reds, the tarmac edged with rough-strewn scree, the exposed rock dull and raw against the elemental sky. This is totally different from the Télégraphe – we have left the vegetation far behind. Peter and Jack set up the summit pit stop, firing up the urn to make some hot chocolate. Even in the sunshine it is bitterly cold. After a week of mountain passes, each with their own characteristics, even after the nonsense that was Ventoux, this feels like the most spectacular and extreme of all. The road wriggles its way down, and we watch the team crawl up the hairpins below. The vista is dauntingly beautiful, the ridge crested with sharply jutting rock, and in the distance we glimpse the snow-capped peak of Mont Blanc.

Mark is first to summit, and looks as though he's having the time of his life. It's one of the best feelings, to have nailed a climb that has been looming large all week, and to know that your fitness has stood up to the test. Always at the back of the mind in anything like this, throughout the preparation and the challenge itself, is the question, can I do it? And it's been an incredibly tough week. Through the vertigo, the atrocious weather, the climbs that seemed endless, it would have been so easy to get into the van and give up. But Mark would never quit. You'd have to cut his legs off to stop him finishing. And now, at the top of the penultimate peak, all the trials fade into insignificance, replaced by the soaring feeling of achievement.

'That was the best climb of the week by far,' he says as he comes to a stop.

'You were looking strong.'

'I feel like I could keep going all day. And the scenery, wow! This is something else.'

Next it's Allen, standing on the pedals to reduce the chafing of the saddle.

'Sore bum, Allen?'

'I can't even begin to tell you,' he says between slightly shallow breaths; at this altitude, the air has noticeably thinned.

Soon JB and Ben come pedalling over the ridge, and we start clapping them in. 'Are we going to sprint it?' JB says, encouraging Ben forwards over the last few metres and letting out a whoop of celebration: 'I'm on top of the world!' He staggers to the altitude sign and leans against it, eyes closed and body sagged in mock or real exhaustion, it's hard to tell. 'Thank god that's over. The highest peak! It's all downhill from here.'

And finally it's Simon, Nobby and Graham. Simon is smiling as usual, though he's clearly struggling. He wraps his cold fingers around a mug of hot chocolate. 'Thanks, Macca,' he says. 'I needed this.'

'You're superstars, all of you,' I say as we gather around the summit sign for the photograph. There's a tangible buzz amongst the group. The Galibier had been looming large all week, and standing at the top, everyone knows the challenge is cracked. Excitement is building. There is just one climb left.

As I look around at the lads, it strikes me how much I have

grown to love this motley crew. Though I knew them before – with the exception of Simon and Graham – I didn't *really* know them. Even JB, a long-term mate, has become a true friend, those long miles of upwards trajectory leading our conversations from the trivial to the profound. Flashbacks of our progress come to me. Getting to know Ben, with each ride finding out yet another job he's had or place he's worked – that boy can't stay still for long. The pride in him we all felt while sharing in his massive weight-loss journey. The moments with Mark; as much as we ribbed him mercilessly, he's priceless, and worked so hard for the Peaky Climbers, always putting in maximum effort. Nobby's quiet confidence, never speaking out of turn, but getting stuck in as much as anyone else, and his superb climbing ability and supportive role which was such an asset to the team. Wrenching Allen out of his shell and finding that incredibly caring, selfless guy underneath who has shown me that it's not always the loudest people who are the most important. Graham's late addition that added so much value in terms of support and expertise, his wife Anna throwing herself into Peaky life just as much as the other partners. It wouldn't have been the same had they not been involved. And Simon, who is almost unrecognisable since this all started. It's not just the physical transformation. His confidence has grown with each peak climbed, and though he was always intelligent, perceptive and genuine, he has become more self-assured, the project giving him and Nicky a new lease of life. He took a gamble on joining the team, and it paid off. More than any other couple, it enhanced their lives.

Over the course of the year the eight of us have become the very best of friends, and we've bonded as a unit, a collection of guys united in their achievement. The year spent in each other's pockets, the fundraising, the training, the exposure of our weaknesses, that's what drew us together and created those bonds. And this final crowning moment, witnessing the team work together this week, has been the most inspiring and humbling experience I've had participating in sport, ever.

Yes, I wish I could have ridden the Galibier with them, and feel that soaring sense of achievement I can now see on each of their faces. But watching them climb these two mountains has been just as satisfying, if not more so, than everything I've personally achieved with the Peaky Climbers. Those who know me from my football days know that I love nothing more than to get a group together, create the right culture, the right mix of personalities, work out how to be successful then execute that plan. So it has been the best of both worlds. For six days we rode as a team side by side, then for the final day I've stood back and looked on as the proudest Englishman in France, witnessing just how special these guys are.

L'Alpe d'Huez is neither the most picturesque nor the most difficult climb of the Tour de France, but it is arguably the most iconic. For the battles that have played out on its slopes, for its being the first peak to host a summit finish, for its being unmistakable in its topography: the road folds back on itself, over and over, in 21 calculated switchbacks. The image from the air looks as though a polygraph has detected an untruth. The climb first featured in the 1952 Tour de France, when the indomitable Italian Fausto Coppi took the stage: 'He's like a cable-car on a steel wire rope,' said Jacques Goddet, Tour director for 50 years. On the 100th anniversary of the Tour, competitors rode it twice. It's a great climb for spectators as, wherever they are, the peloton can be seen slowly creeping up the hairpins below. Thousands of riders attempt the climb each week in the summer months. This was one of the peaks that was on the original list when the challenge was first conceived. Not riding is not an option.

It's a decision that will contribute to my not being able to walk for weeks after the challenge is over, and not to be able to ride a bike for months. With torn hamstrings, damaged patella, inflamed ligaments and ripped muscles, I will sit static and frustrated while the rest of the team go out for a leisurely spin, re-living their Peaky Climber glory. But there is not one person on this team who has found it easy. Every single one has reached their limit and pushed through; each has dug deeper than we ever dreamed we would need to. This is about the Peaky Climbers, a team greater than the sum of its parts, that has pushed and sweated and trained and strained for 12 long months, that has achieved what others told us was impossible, and that has reached the final peak of this ridiculous challenge.

The famous 21 hairpins of the Alpe d'Huez are all that stand between us and the end of our journey. I have to do this.

We have arranged to meet our wives, partners, friends and sponsors in Bourg-d'Oisans, the town nestled at the foot of the famous climb, and for 40 cold and painful kilometres we ride, the peloton abuzz with adrenaline, the guys carrying me along in the centre of it all. Emotions run high as we close in on the bustling market town, rolling down narrow streets lined with the patisseries, gift shops and restaurants that serve the many tourists and cyclists who appear in the busy summer months. It's typically continental, with awnings, outdoor seating, pavement cafés and bunting strung across the street. Then there they are, a crowd of familiar faces gathered outside one of the cafés, bursting into applause as they catch sight of us, striking up with 'We love you Peakies, we do!' There follow brief but meaningful exchanges; since we last saw each other we have been through so much.

Being reunited with our partners bursts the challenge wide open. It is the culmination of the week, during which we rode our personal challenges and struggled as a team. It is the culmination of the year, where eight families made sacrifices in their own way, eight individual journeys that have converged at the foot of this mountain.

We found out later that the support team were shocked at how awful we looked. Expecting jubilant faces they were taken by surprise at our sunken cheeks, the prominent lines, the huge bags beneath the eyes, the grey pallor clinging to our skin. 'Steve said you looked like you'd spent the week in Belsen,' Nicola later told me.

The Alpe d'Huez towers over the town, an immense, vertical slab taking up half the sky. It looks more difficult from this perspective than any of the climbs we've scaled so far. Nicola looks a bit shocked. 'Tell me you haven't been climbing mountains like that all week,' she says.

I chuckle. 'That one definitely looks the worst, but yeah, they've all been mad.'

'Wow. I had no idea.'

She looks awed, something I might once have played on, trying to impress my wife by how tough I was. But all that is over. It's not about beating this challenge, or assuming we have any kind of elevated status, or having any sense of conquering anything. In this moment, surrounded by the loved ones who have got us here, it is about their support, their belief and love. I give her a hug and a kiss. Cycling widow? No chance.

It's not long before we must continue. 'Come on, Peaky Climbers, it's time to get moving. One last climb.' We mount our bicycles and push away from the bustling street, wolf-whistles and cheers echoing in our wake. Straight away we hit the climb, then shortly afterwards pass the sign numbering the first hairpin. Above, the road swings steadily back and forth in an effort to move man and beast up this impossible mountain.

Behind, we hear engines approaching and a siren wailing.

'Is that the police?' JB asks.

'You must have forgotten to pay the bill for your tart-de-custard,' says Simon.

The noise draws closer and a window is rolled down, then a voice yells, 'Come on you Peaky Climbers!' It's our support team, and they pass us whooping, cheering and banging on the doors. Clive in the next car has brought a loud speaker, and his wife Sam hollers through it as they pass. 'Don't hit them!' shrieks Nicola from the passenger seat as a driver approaches in the oncoming lane and the cavalcade is squashed into our lane. They match our pace for a while – 'Get out the way!' they tease – then drive on.

Allen laughs as they disappear around the next bend. 'They are mad!' We are all pumped. Slowly and steadily we tick off the hairpins as the racket echoes from above. Every so often they stop, and as we approach they ramp up the volume, cheering and yelling encouragement, horns and music blaring. The refrain of 'We love you Peakies, we do,' repeats again and again. We truly feel as though we're part of the Tour de France and we bask in the attention. None of us could ever forget such a moment.

With the boost from our family and friends these seven could have flown up, even Ben who is somewhat broken after the Galibier, and they're all itching to finish, but everyone is sticking to my sluggish pace, one final act of the Peaky team ethic. It's an unbearable grind, and for 12 long kilometres the tactic is to grit teeth, keep spinning, and don't stop. With every pedal stroke I utter an expletive. 'I didn't know your cussing could get even worse!' Allen says.

With two kilometres to go, the chalets and restaurants of the resort appear, the ski lifts incongruous on the green slopes. A solitary bar is open but other than that everything is deserted. We have been steadily rising for two hours and are now nearly level with the surrounding peaks, the whole Oisans valley spread out below, the town radiating outwards from its centre. Down the mountainside are the unmistakable bends up which we have crawled. Peter and Jack are waiting with the vans on the final corner, just out of sight of the finish line, and we stop to regroup. The decision was made months ago that, whatever happened during these seven days, we would finish together. A few words said, some hugs and high fives, then it's up, over the brow and onto the final 200m stretch.

There's a strange silence among the team, an unusual absence of comments as we reflect on what we are on the verge of achieving. I suddenly get the sense of floating above, lifted by the adrenaline, and it's no longer me at the pedals, but instead I'm looking down at an extraordinary team of cyclists, some with heads bowed, some with faces smiling, all with legs spinning, surging forwards as one. It seems a lifetime ago that we sat in the Fox at our first team meeting, everyone making the acquaintance of everyone else, exchanging nervous laughter, this moment a vague blur in an imagined future.

Our bunch spreads out so we are riding side by side, and there appears our destination, the centre of the ski resort, the *Arrivée Tour de France* sign, and ribbons stretched across the road, with our entire entourage cheering, singing and hollering support. A cacophony fires up. Each person is blowing on a plastic whistle, lifting the party to ever more raucous heights as we approach our finish line. We're all grinning, laughing, pushing forwards, and I shout 'steady', and 'keep in line,' to the guys. JB raises his fist as we draw closer. The whole support team has donned feather boas in addition to their woolly hats, and they clutch balloons and bottles of champagne as the whistles grow ever louder.

This is the moment that had been at the back of all of our minds when we first signed on the dotted line, the moment of completion that would mean we had achieved what we'd set out to do. The trials that we'd been through to get here, all the times it looked as though we might not make it, the bodies screaming at us to stop, the exhaustion, the mental effort, the weather, the roads, the near-misses, the zooming descents, the overshot corners, the never quite crashing. But wow, what a seven days it's been. The scenery, the climbs, the digging deep, the sense of achievement, the camaraderie, the support we've given each other, the dedication that every single person has put in. It's a real band of brothers who are completing this challenge. I look down the line, my heart bursting with pride as we cross the finish line as we started: together.

The road is wet with champagne. Bottles are passed around with no need for glasses. Everyone is grinning inanely. The hugs begin, the kisses, the congratulations. Exhausted, shell-shocked and elated, we work our way around the group so we can share this moment with everyone, taking our time; at last, there is no rush. Stumbling to the summit stone we crowd around for our final mountaintop photograph, then everyone piles in, wives, girlfriends, sponsors. Mark is on Simon's shoulders. The triumph is uninhibited.

'Speech! Speech!' Somehow, they want me to say something. Oh God. Overwhelmed with pain and emotion, I have no words. I want to thank everyone, who from the beginning of this journey has made it happen in their small way. It's impossible to process what we've just done. The sense of occasion is too much; my voice breaks as I try to speak, and I wipe away the tears as I look around at the assembled group, who are also welling up. With cycle helmet in one hand and champagne in the other I manage to garble a few thank yous. 'Thanks for believing in us. Allez the Peaky Climbers!'

Later we will drive to a nearby Chateau where the party will rage for the next two nights. There will be bubbly and endless speeches, almost everyone taking their turn to say something, and there will be tears, laughter, and the usual banter. Allen will take his first drink for a year. The high of having completed the challenge has settled deep upon everyone. Simon looks as though he will never come down.

We really did it. We really climbed all those mountains, just a bunch of average guys, and we really raised all that money, which will make a tangible difference to real people's lives. It was an outlandish, ridiculous idea, and people said we couldn't do it. Christ, even Chris Hoy said we were mad. But we did it. All because we dared to give it a try.

Before we know it, it will be Sunday evening and we'll be back in Blighty, bumping back down to earth and real life. It's happened; it's done. What now? Bodies broken, spirits soaring.

Recovering over the following weeks, focussing on everything that's been neglected for a year, then depression, missing the team, all of our followers already moving on to the next big thing. But this is something that can never be forgotten. It takes time for our appetites to abate, and the flashbacks and disbelief last for months. Already we are questioning, 'How do we top that?' Because something has started, and at some point in the future we know there will be another Peaky challenge.

The cold sun fades as the day grows older, and as the congratulations ring through the deserted resort, the dying light touches the tips of the surrounding peaks, snow-topped and edged with orange. There is one last explosion of colour as the sun is extinguished, drawing this final day to a close. What an adventure. What's next?

The original eight ready to ascend the Tumble for the first time.
L-R (back) Paul, Nobby, Ben, Cricky (front) JB, Stuart, Allen, Simon.

Looking like pros at the airport, ready for the challenge ahead.
L-R Nobby, Cricky, JB, Paul, Allen, Ben, Graham, Simon.

Terrible weather on day one. The team rides through the rain.

Lining up to take the first summit, Hautacam.
L-R Ben, Allen, Simon, Paul, Nobby, JB, Cricky, Graham.

Joined at the hip: Cricky and Nobby climb Luz Ardiden.

Larking around at summit no. 2, Luz Ardiden.
L-R Graham, Simon, Cricky, Allen, Paul, JB, Ben, Nobby.

The gruesome twosome, pairs Allen and Ben.

Stunning views and tough climbs: the team snake up the mountainside.

Summit selfie.
L-R Nobby, Cricky, JB, Ben, Simon, Allen, Graham, Paul (taking the photo).

Eating is just as much of a challenge as the riding: empty plates and full bellies.
L-R Jack (Le Domestique), Graham, Cricky, Peter (Le Domestique), JB, Allen,
Simon, Ben, Nobby.

Crazy amounts of snow on the Tourmalet summit.
L-R (back) Graham, Simon, JB, Paul, Allen, Nobby (front) Ben, Cricky.

Enough of the rain! A tedious climb up the Col de Menté.
L-R Graham, Cricky, Ben, Allen, Paul, Nobby, Simon, JB.

Partners in crime Paul and JB on the first climb of Ventoux.

After three ascents and a full day of climbing the same mountain, the Peaky Climbers celebrate becoming Cinglés du Mont Ventoux – the madmen of Ventoux. L-R Allen, Simon, JB, Graham, Paul, Nobby, Ben, (front) Cricky.

A 50th birthday to remember: cycling up mountains all day with a bunch of crazy buffoons! L-R Nobby, JB, Ben, Paul, Allen, Simon, Graham, Cricky.

"Riding your bike doesn't get much better than this." A beautiful ride up the Homme Mort for steadfast pair Simon and Graham.

A long day's ride ends with a blistering sunset.

Grey skies return for the Ornon summit, but team spirit shines through.
L-R Nobby, Graham, Simon, Ben, Cricky, JB, Allen, Paul.

Graham suffers at the Glandon summit.

Relief that the climb is over on the freezing cold Glandon summit.
L-R Paul, Ben, Nobby, Cricky, Allen, Simon, Graham, JB.

Pumped for the final day but missing the team skipper.
L-R Peter (Le Domestique), Cricky, Graham, Ben, Allen, Nobby, Simon, JB,
Jack (Le Domestique).

"It's downhill from here" JB relieved to hit the top of the biggest
peak of the week.

Emotional reunions in Bourg-d'Oisans: Paul and Nicola.

Allen and Kirstie in Bourg-d'Oisans.

*The wives and girlfriends wait for the team on the Alpe d'Huez.
L-R Anna Cherrill, Kirstie Stacey, Nicky McIntosh, Mandy Boaler, Catherine
Lambert, Nicky Haly, Jane Barson, Jane Crick.*

Speech! Emotions run high now the challenge is over.

The team, wives, girlfriends and supporters at the top of the Alpe d'Huez.

In their own words

Neil "Nobby" Barson

Our challenge has finally come to an end, and what a challenge it proved to be. Thankfully we dedicated a year of our lives to train hard in all weathers because boy, did we need to dig deep. Although we had the most horrendous weather I felt it made this crazy challenge even more enormous. I feel very proud and honoured to have been part of such a fantastic team, who have now become great friends. I think the most memorable thing about the seven days in the saddle isn't about me or the amazing scenery, it's the respect I have for all the Peakies. Seeing some of the boys going through the pain barrier and beyond to complete every climb really was inspirational. Thank you Peakies for the past year of blood, sweat and tears. Bring on our next challenge.

Mark "Cricky" Crick

I'm left with a huge hole to fill; however, I now feel part of something very special and I believe my team mates feel the same. I also feel amazingly honoured to have been part of such a life changing experience. It has also taught me humility and respect for team instructions.

Allen Stacey

The ride was tough but we always knew it would be. The sense of achievement I got from completing the challenge is massive, but the sense of achievement I got from being part of a team that raised so much money for the charities to make a difference to people's lives was even bigger.

John 'JB' Boaler

I am quite lost for words after what we have experienced over both the last week and indeed the last year. The teamwork that has got us through this immense challenge, both in training and the event itself, has been quite amazing. I can't say the event itself was all enjoyable, it was extremely tough at times, but we got each other through it with great humour and it meant we all enjoyed the amazing scenery and the buzz. I also felt we were supported in the dark times by all the people who are not with us anymore.

Then there is the support we received from partners, sponsors, friends (including all the Facebook likes) and family. The last climb into Alpe d'Huez was particularly special, with the supporters cheering us on as if we were actually in the Tour de France itself.

It has been quite amazing. Thank you, Macca, for insisting I be involved in this event and part of an incredible group of people.

Simon Haly

As I retrace my steps through the past 12 months, although the event seemed to come around quickly, I don't really know how we managed to cram everything in, and more importantly I can confirm that all eight of us are still happily married, which is a testament to the loyalty and support from our partners, friends and extended family.

I think we all probably thought that the actual tour would be a welcome relief from the typical English summer weather but boy, were we in for a surprise. Not in my wildest dreams did I expect to rue the mistake of thinking I wouldn't need my winter gloves when packing for the trip. It was probably the best and worst weather I have ever experienced but this has just made it a more memorable experience. My highlights were going over the top of the Tourmalet in snow, completing the ascent of the Col de la Croix de Fer in freezing wet conditions and obviously all crossing the finishing line as one team with our family and friends cheering us on. The support we have received over the past year has astounded me and continues to do so when I meet someone and they say they followed us throughout the tour and offer huge congratulations for what we have achieved – I am always somewhat humbled and proud.

I could not have completed the year or Tour without the constant support of my now lifelong cycling friends, who have made me laugh on so many occasions, have dragged me up so many hills and mountains, and have never moaned when squandering the chance of a PB on Strava. I thank Macca for the chance to be included in 'The Peaky Climbers' and hope that the group will continue to cycle, raise charity money and have fun!

Graham Cherrill

Obviously, a bit different for me only coming in at three months, but I enjoyed getting the sponsorship together, getting out with each of you for rides, and starting to get to know you all, so knew what to expect.

I enjoyed sitting in with Ben or Simon chatting and being about just in case; hopefully the ongoing waffle kept them company! They did tremendously well and deserved it after the year they'd put in.

These multi-day events are always longer days than anyone plans but never felt particularly rushed, and the evenings were good relaxed fun.

Favourite bit has to be coming up the Tourmalet with Si dodging the snow plough.

I'm not a nostalgic person who looks back at stuff, I'm always looking at the next thing, but this time I took a week off the bike, looked back at the rides and photos and took in what had happened.

I can say that I made the right decision to come on board, witness what you guys achieved in 12 months, the realisation of what a difference that sum of money will provide and know that I have helped in a little way. It has all been an experience to treasure.

Ben Heavers

Wow, what a journey, from the moment Macca asked if I was interested in a cycling challenge, to increasing the cycling training with sportives and trips with the team. Heading out to the Isle of Wight to work with the kids of Caring Cancer Trust and meeting the team of The British Lung Foundation at Ride London. A roller coaster of emotions. A few days before leaving on our epic journey I had this feeling of just wanting to get going but a few nerves at what was coming and the unknown.

I don't think any of us knew what was coming...the first couple of days' weather started with cold rain but the views were insane. Once at the top of these mountains the views of the surrounding landscapes took your breath away. We encountered snow, rain, wind and one day with amazing sunshine, but no matter the weather it was such an incredible sense of achievement and knowing we'd raised so much for two brilliant charities.

The whole trip was loaded with emotions but the last

day our wives, partners, sponsors and my parents had made the trip to see us finish. To see all their faces as we came round the last corner brought the challenge to life. The support was amazing. I can honestly say I have never done anything before like this, but whatever Macca suggests next, I'm there.

Anna acknowledgements

Firstly, congratulations to the Peaky Climbers team for completing the challenge and raising all that money. What an achievement! It has been a pleasure learning about your journey and sharing your story.

Thanks to Paul for asking me to be part of the process of turning the story into a book. Many thanks to all the people who contributed material: the team, Steve Aram, Robert Cartledge (Le Domestique Tours), Bob Haly and Clive Robson. Thanks for responding to my questions, and apologies that I couldn't fit all of it in!

Thank you to Simon Warren for your excellent work producing the graphics of the climbs.

Thanks to the following for test-reading early drafts of the book and providing honest and insightful feedback: Stephanie Budd, Heidi Chilton, Chris Dent, Sarah Frecknall, Anne Robinson, Hannah Schneider, Alan Spence and Martyn Wells. Particular thanks to David Ardill and Clifton Hughes who gave up their time and expertise to help shape the manuscript, and extra special thanks to Cathy Bussey who did a terrific job as editor.

Paul acknowledgements

I will start my acknowledgements with two people who didn't cycle one bit, didn't personally raise a penny but without whom this incredible story would not have been told.

My Mum, Valerie Gwen Mary McIntosh, died far too young at the age of 68 from an awful lung disease called Idiopathic Pulmonary Fibrosis. There's still no cure (at the time of writing), it was awful for her and our family, but her life was inspirational to me and my siblings. A woman of diminutive stature, but who packed a real punch. She played football the way she lived life – aggressively. For me, she inspires me still and was the reason I dreamt up this crazy idea in the first place.

Then there was the wonderful, the beautiful Maisie Norton. The delicate flower, who my son fell in love with, but who had armour of steel. She was diagnosed with cancer at the tender age of 11 but that only fuelled her fire to live a full and incredible life. My family were blessed to know her, along with everyone in and around Wantage and the local area. She inspired like-minded children with similar experiences. Her wonderful parents, Steve and Rosie, and sister Ellie and brother Owen, have been through things none of us will ever experience. Maisie and the Norton family are the other inspiration behind the Peaky Climbers.

When I came up with this idea, I ran it by some dear friends who believed in me enough to provide corporate sponsorship: Clive and Sam Robson (Bellwood Projects) and Steve Aram and Suzanne Dalgleish (VTech Systems Ltd), without whom this challenge would never have got off the ground. Any inspiration and idea needs believers, and these guys believed from day one, then supported the team the whole way through, and for that I will be forever thankful. To our other corporate sponsors I say a huge thank you: Nick Sheehan and Gary Houghton from iLine, Andrew Durkin at MustardPR, David Lock at Vuzix and the team at LA Vision for sponsoring us and for believing.

My Peaky Climbers team mates. Words cannot express my undying love, admiration and heartfelt thanks for everything they have sacrificed to change not only my life but those who have benefited from the huge sums of money they have raised. Simon Haly, Allen Stacey, Ben Heavers, Graham Cherrill, John Boaler, Mark Crick and Neil Barson are what legends are made of. While I hope this book conveys their depth of commitment, sacrifice, desire and passion, I'm sure only the movie can really do that! All of our lives have changed. 'It's more than just a cycle ride, it's a way of life' – that's true for all of us now.

My family. Wow, I won the lottery when I met Nicola. We

then had two wonderful kids, Jai and Ethan. They have always supported my hair-brained ideas, been there when I have tried to do this, that and the other, at work or personally. I just could not have done any of this challenge without their total, undying support or Nicky's amazing flapjack. An eternal thank you to each of them.

Then there's Jane, Jane, Catherine, Kirstie, Nicky, Mandy and Anna, and Nicola of course. Our wives and partners who I'm sure never realised what their other halves were getting into but who supported us every single second of every single day, through the great times, tough rides, crazy diets and all the events to raise money for our chosen charities. Eight incredible women, plus all those around supporting them, who were just as incredible as the Peaky Climbers. We eight could not have done it without those eight.

Our two chosen charities are both very special. From The Caring Cancer Trust, Ian MacWatt and Chris Ody plus all the team do an incredible job of supporting the children who have experienced cancer and giving them the opportunity of getting together and talking through their experiences. From the British Lung Foundation, the team led by Penny Woods were fantastically supportive, so a huge thank you to Jason Cater, Rebekah Ahmed, Katie Lyall, Alison, Esther and Chris and also Kirsty Whipp who really supported and believed from day one.

Thank you to Kevin Keegan for taking my random call, and Chris Hoy, Angela Rippon and all those famous people who held the Peaky Climbers card and voiced the fact we were nuts. To Le Domestique for their support over the seven day challenge, to our coaches, to Steve Davidson at the Fox in Denchworth for accommodating all our meetings and the wonderful Wayne Smith for managing our meetings. To Nicky Henshall for her unswerving support, Mike Nickituk for his generosity, and C U Tuesdays for being the best local band. To Bob Haly for the surprise visit on day six and to Lesley Burton for managing to snare photos with famous people. I just can't namecheck everyone; if I could I would, and if I've missed you out you know I love you!

A very special thank you to Anna Hughes for helping us write this book. She was prepared to listen, she really understood what we'd achieved and without her this book would not be in your hands now. Thank you, Anna.

And many thanks to you for buying, borrowing, stealing or listening to this book, the proceeds of which are going to our two wonderful charities. We hope to inspire people of a similar age and waistline to get up and get out and absolutely believe they can take on and achieve something amazing. Just go for it.

Love to Mum and Maisie…now and always x

The Peaky Climbers' adventures will continue.

Follow the team and their next crazy challenge at

www.peakyclimbers.com